EASY TAROT GUIDE

by Marcia Masino

THE WORLD.

THE MAGICIAN.

PENTACLES.

STRENGTH.

WHEEL of FORTUNE.

KING of SWORDS.

International Standard Book Number 0-917086-59-7

Cover Design by Barbara Bethea

Rider-Waite Tarot cards reproduced by permission of
U.S. Games Systems, Inc., New York 10016.
Copyright 1971 by U.S. Games Systems, Inc.
Further reproduction prohibited.

Printed in Singapore
by Toppan Printing Co. (S) Pte Ltd.

Published by ACS Publications, Inc.
P.O. Box 34487
San Diego, CA 92103-0802

First Printing, November 1987
Second Printing, September 1988
Third Printing, November 1989

Dedication

For my teachers, and that includes everyone.

Contents

Preface

Tarot cards first entered my life in my teenage years. I was drawn to their power to predict the future. (I am a Scorpio, with Saturn, the Midheaven and Mercury in that sign.) When a reader performed two correct readings for me, I became inspired to persevere with my own deck and to attempt divining.

I studied a few books, but learned to read Tarot mostly by practical experience with the public. That experience taught me as no book ever could. During that same year I had begun my professional career, and the organization I worked for demanded that my work be correct. That was a challenge, as I was reading publicly with masses of people waiting their turn and limited to 10 minutes each. From there I quickly went into business with my partner Anne Toth. It was then that the mystery of the Tarot began to unfold. I interpreted the cards' messages, taught and continued studying.

The *Easy Tarot Guide* has evolved from my experiences of teaching Tarot reading over the past years. It is a basic introductory text. Learning the Tarot independently has been a frustration for many individuals. Sincere students find themselves in a quandary concerning details and practical questions, and need instruction. The lessons in the *Easy Tarot Guide*, therefore, have been designed in a format so students can check their progress. I've attempted to anticipate and answer commonly asked questions. Whether studying independently or with a group, students will obtain successful, practical, immediate results.

Language is power. Studies indicate that people reading the generic "he" or "man" usually visualize a male human being, rather than both sexes. In order to include all humans, this book shall alternate masculine and feminine pronouns. Thus, some areas will use he, him, his and himself, while other areas will use she, her, hers and herself. Both sets of pronouns are intended to be "generic" — to include the entire human race.

Since the Major Arcana **Judgement** tarot card in the Rider-Waite deck, is spelled with an "e," that is the spelling used in *Easy Tarot*; rather than "Judgment," which is today's preferred spelling in the United States.

Consulting the cards can be very informative. Studying their deeper, esoteric content will be enlightening. Living and becoming these energies is direct illumination.

Marcia Masino
March, 1984

Acknowledgments

A very special thank-you to Anne S. Toth, who respected, loved and believed in me. Her gift of spirit, courage and intelligence shall always be one of my greatest sources of strength.

Gratitude to Barbara Michael, who patiently and unselfishly transformed my unintelligible handwritten scribbles into a beautiful, meticulously typed manuscript.

Appreciation to my parents, friends, family and students, who gave continual encouragement, were "sure the book would be accepted," and were just as excited as I when it was.

Introduction

The Tarot's real history is almost hidden, just as are the meanings of the cards.

Stuart R. Kaplan wrote that the Tarot cards, "conceal the profound knowledge of antiquity..." and that it is not known..."whether the Major and Minor Arcana were created together, or took form each born of separate genius."[1] What is seen in the symbology of the Tarot is from one's own intuition — thus knowledge is imparted for self-awareness.

This book, having been designed as a workbook for learning the Tarot — thus the title *Easy Tarot Guide*, will be a continuous reference even after you have learned how to perform a reading.

Remarkable interpretative results can be obtained when you get involved immediately with the Tarot deck's pictures.

The Rider-Waite Tarot deck has been chosen for this book. This deck is easily obtainable and its complete symbolism is excellent. I suggest you begin your Tarot adventure with the Rider-Waite deck and branch out into other decks later.

Spread the entire 78-card pack on a large table. Have all the cards facing the same direction — upright towards those who will be viewing them.

After the cards are placed on the table, take a good, long look at them. Notice which ones you find drawing your attention, the ones you come back to again and again. (This exercise should take from five to ten minutes.)

The idea of this exercise is to base your selection solely on the emotional appeal they have for you. You may be drawn to the picture, symbols, color or design of the card. All of these are fine reasons for your choices. Do not pick the card you "always choose" unless it really appeals to you this time.

You can read the name of a card in the Minor Arcana by looking at its suit; Wands, Cups, Swords or Pentacles and the Roman numeral it bears. The symbol for the suit will be in the picture and the numeral is usually at the top. On a Court card, the member of the Court is depicted by a King, Queen, Knight or Page.

You can identify a card in the Major Arcana by the Roman numeral at the top and the title on the bottom, e.g., The Star, The Hermit, and so on.

Record the 2, 3 or 4 cards you find attractive or drawing your attention. Make sure you've looked the cards over thoroughly.

---

1. Stuart R. Kaplan, *The Encyclopedia of Tarot*, New York: U.S. Games Systems, Inc., 1978.

Cards I Am Attracted To

Card 1 _____ Meaning _____
Card 2 _____ Meaning _____
Card 3 _____ Meaning _____
Card 4 _____ Meaning _____
Date _____

To find the meanings of the cards, turn to Part III, Card Interpretations.

You will find that the cards you have chosen are relevant to your present life conditions. Your favorite cards will describe your present circumstances physically, mentally, emotionally and spiritually. They may represent present involvements, goals or aspects of your life that you are concerned with and working on. When a Court card is chosen, it can represent a person in your life or the personality traits it depicts can be qualities you are using or striving to cultivate and express.

Now record 2 or 3 cards that you dislike or find repulsive.

Cards I Dislike

Card 1 _____ Meaning _____
Card 2 _____ Meaning _____
Card 3 _____ Meaning _____
Card 4 _____ Meaning _____
Date _____

Again turn to the interpretation section and write in the cards' meanings.

The cards you dislike reveal parts of your life that make you unhappy or cause you distress. Often such cards indicate areas that you dislike handling or you avoid altogether.

What draws us to one card and not another and why does this card, when interpreted, make sense? How can we pick cards that have significance in our lives when we don't know their meanings?

The answer is the Tarot card's symbols. Although we don't consciously know their meanings, we subconsciously recognize these symbols and even their significance. Imbedded in the subconscious mind is a world of symbolism. Some of us compose, write and paint in this language of symbols. We also dream in this language. Through it our dreams communicate about our past, our present, and yes, sometimes even hint at our future. Often a dream is recalled because the subconscious is trying to get through to us to help us deal with a situation, trying to give us insight, reasoning or awareness. The dream is often meaningless until interpreted. The Tarot uses a different approach to invoke these images sleeping in our subconscious. Instead of interpreting a dream, we interpret the symbolism of the cards as representing our past, present and future.

No one lives a pain-free, totally happy life. The more we understand about how and why things happen, however, the more likelihood of lessening our pain and increasing our happiness. The insights of Tarot are offered within this book for that purpose.

Statements about interpretations should **not** be taken as absolutes. The future has a degree of flux. Many times, we do not know how much of a difference we can have in matters, until we try. It is our hope that the theories within this book will motivate the seeker to find alternatives, to search out options which can overcome possible "unhappy endings" and ameliorate potential difficulties.

Thus, if cards caution about health, financial restrictions or other unwanted unpleasantness, we hope the reader will take that information as an impetus to make changes (in attitudes and actions) to create the most positive outcomes possible. We believe that all of us have within us the power to change our lives for the better.

When we realize that our subconscious remembers our past, reflects our present and deduces as well as divines our future, then the mechanics of what goes on in a Tarot interpretation becomes more clear. Include the mystery and magic of these romantic, esoteric symbols, and the story is complete.

PART I
DECK DESCRIPTION

THE MINOR ARCANA INTRODUCED

Included in the Tarot deck is a group of cards divided into four suits: Wands (sometimes titled Rods), Swords, Cups and Pentacles (Disks or Coins).

The playing deck of cards used today originated from these four suits. The Wands became Clubs, Swords became Spades, Cups became Hearts and Pentacles became Diamonds. Each of the four suits is numbered Ace through Ten, with the addition of the Court cards: King, Queen, Knight and Page. These 10 cards per suit (Ace through Ten), times four suits, equal 40 cards. The 16 Court cards (four per suit times the four suits) plus the 40 number cards (Ace — Ten in each suit times the four suits) bring this group to a total of 56 cards.

This 56 card grouping is called the Minor Arcana. The word *arcanaum* (plural *arcana*) means hidden or secret knowledge and information of the spiritual, psychological worlds. The Minor Arcana depict conditions and circumstances in daily life. In this part of the Tarot we see events and situations that comprise our personal world and its experiences.

The Court cards are the people in our lives and how we affect them and they, us. They are the individuals that influence and participate in our personal world of existence.

Find the Minor Arcana in your Tarot deck and place them on a table. Remember; you should have 56 cards, Ace through Ten plus the 16 Court cards. The number cards (Ace — Ten) show pictures of events. For example, the Six of Cups depicts children and their home; the Four of Pentacles shows a man and his money, and so on. Each number card expresses a different aspect of our lives, each Court card represents the personality of the various people in our lives.

Now lay just the suit of Wands out in front of you and see what kind of events are going on. Here are people achieving, defending, fighting and competing. The cards of this suit represent the competitive, ambitious, creative, enterprising, determined and energetic aspects of our lives. The characters in this suit, including the court, are concerned with their goals, enterprises, growth and aims in life and success. Additional qualities of Wands are energy, courage, initiative, enthusiasm and adventure seeking.

Try to find a card in the suit of Wands representing:

1. Victory concerning goals _____

2. Overwork, over-ambitious _____

3. Fighting _____

4. Defending _____

5. Looking forward toward new enterprises and their results _____

The people of this suit (Court cards) have personalities similar to the qualities we use for the rest of the suit. They are ambitious, energetic, creative, courageous and enterprising. Astrologically, the Wands suit corresponds to the element fire and the fire signs of Aries, Sagittarius and Leo. You may know people born under these signs who remind you of the Wands Court cards. Those born with a large distribution of planets in the fire signs may also express these fiery tendencies.

The suit of Cups is next. Lay them out on a table and discover what feelings the pictures convey. You will notice they are distinctly different from the suit of Wands. The Cups deal with the emotional aspects of life, showing events surrounding our loved ones and the giving and receiving of love. We see family, romance, relationships and the ups and downs of our emotional lives.

Try to find a card in the suit of Cups representing:

1. Family _____

2. Retreat _____

3. Celebration _____

4. Romance _____

5. Loss of love _____

The Cups suit depicts emotions and love, dreams and imagination, creative and artistic talents and enjoyment of the family and social aspects of life. The water signs of Pisces, Cancer and Scorpio are shown in this suit. See if you can find water used as a symbol in this suit and look for fish and sea-creatures incorporated into the symbolism.

The next suit is Swords. Laying them out will reveal yet another type of life's experiences. Conditions of strife prevail, with scenes of loss, suffering and defeat. See if you can locate some positive Swords cards, ones that suggest triumph over obstacles or relief from difficulties:

1. Victory or triumph over obstacles _____

2. Movement away from difficulties _____

3. Retreat for peace of mind _____

4. Indecision _____

In the suit of Swords, problems and difficulties are major themes. Here we find actions, sometimes cruel, revengeful, unfair and malicious. Also, there are scenes of retaliation, separation, loss and bondage as a result of these painful dilemmas. You may be thinking that some of these problems could be in a person's own mind, causing suffering and fears. Sometimes this is true, but nonetheless the result is person's mental anguish. The Swords cards can suggest mental cruelty, confusion and calculation of revengeful plans. This is the suit of the mind — the conscious mind and intellect. Mind is symbolized by the sword, for it is double-edged, suggesting our thoughts are equally dual in character — imprisoning us through our outlook or freeing us through the use of right thinking and positive attitude. In the Swords suit both the right and wrong use of action and attitude are expressed, along with the positive or negative results. The air signs of Gemini, Libra and Aquarius are represented in this suit. Look for air and wind to be strongly represented in the symbolism, as well as air creatures.

The Pentacles suit deals with the practical, realistic, material aspects of life. It indicates income; how we earn, handle and invest monies; and ownership of property and possessions. Business, job training, mastery and work recognition are also shown. All these categories are practical in nature, dealing with everyday, tangible things; therefore, the Coins or Pentacles, also solid objects of value and worth, symbolize this suit. Pentacles involve the financial measurement of the energy we put into our jobs, life's work and our material position.

Try to find a card in the suit of Pentacles representing:

1. Sharing of the prosperity _____
2. Holding on to money _____
3. Juggling and adjusting monies _____
4. Financial loss _____
5. Wealth _____

The earth sign people of Taurus, Virgo and Capricorn belong to the Pentacles suit. Look for goat and bull symbols in the Court cards.

Now look at the Court cards alone. As noted above, the Wands Court cards show ambitious people, enthusiastic and adventurous in nature. The Cups Court people have loved ones on their minds, and are sympathetic, emotional, sensitive and feeling. These individuals are the imaginative ones of the Court, the romantics. Swords entities often have a history of personal trials and tribulations that have made them either incredibly strong, filled with power and determination, or bitter and resentful, living in the past. Their minds are their blessing or their curse; mental attitudes can make or break their lives. Decisiveness, intelligence, mental challenges, insights, fair-mindedness, humanitarianism, rights and communication are all qualities at which they excel. Pentacles people measure life through tangible things such as what they own and earn. Possessions are important, as is a well-paying job. They are the workers of the court, willing to plug along toward these goals with persistence and determination.

All Tarot cards have different meanings when they are RE-VERSED (fall upside down).

On the negative side of the Court personalities, we find the Wands characters can be willful, selfish, pushy, arrogant, jealous, argumentative and sometimes violent.

The Cups Court cards have great imaginations that they use to create romantic dreams and artistic projects. When these people show up reversed in a reading, their fantasizing may run away with them, causing them to imagine all sorts of hurts and slights. They can become overly sensitive, or allow a morbid imagination to cause doubts, insecurities, suspicions and worries, to the point of becoming self-destructive and self-defeating. The Cups people may have a hard time forgetting the past. They see situations through an emotional haze.

The Swords natives suffer but survive, often through their own willpower and determination, surprising themselves at their own mental powers. Often they regard the sorrow incurred as a crisis point in their lives, causing them to call upon their own resources and turning a negative into a positive. The Swords peoples' downfall is the inability to overcome the loss, turning bitter and inward. Having suffered and lost, they can wet-blanket another's good fortune, expecting the worst and filling other's minds with suspicion and mistrust. When these Court cards appear reversed in a reading, be careful of embittered attitudes, turning pleasure into confusion. They can become prejudiced, filled with accusations that are based not on facts but suspicions, and make threats based on these prejudices. They incline to sarcasm, cynicism, criticism, excess severity and judging too harshly (including themselves).

Pentacles individuals can become too possessive, looking at their loved ones as objects rather than individuals. Greed, illegitimate dealings with money, financial carelessness, overdependence, worry, status-seeking, nit-picking and selfish manipulation of money matters are all possible qualities of character.

Review of the Minor Arcana

MATCHING
Match the name of the suit in the left column with its correct meaning in the right column.

_____ 1. Wands   a. Imagination, emotions, love
_____ 2. Cups   b. Money, job, reality
_____ 3. Swords   c. Ideas, ambition, competition
_____ 4. Pentacles   d. Mind, difficulties, actions and reactions concerning problems

TRUE OR FALSE
_____ 1. There are 56 cards in the entire Tarot deck.
_____ 2. The playing deck of cards we use today was derived from the Tarot.
_____ 3. In the Minor Arcana we find the Court cards and the suits (Aces-Tens).
_____ 4. There are four suits and four Court cards for each suit.
_____ 5. The Court cards show pictures of events that happen in our daily lives.
_____ 6. The Minor cards, Aces-Tens of each suit, are the people that have these events happening to them.
_____ 7. Wands — activities are enterprising, outgoing, driven.
_____ 8. Cups — deal with the family and love given and received.
_____ 9. Swords — are associated with finances, possessions and work.
_____ 10. Pentacles — indicate practical, material matters.
_____ 11. The Court cards of the suit of Pentacles represent people who are artistic, emotional dreamers.
_____ 12. The Swords people use their minds as their weapons.
_____ 13. The Wands Court people are plodders, workers and possessive.
_____ 14. The Cups people care about mental challenges, decision-making and justice.
_____ 15. The Wands court cards have their minds on loved ones and feelings.
_____ 16. Pentacles = thinking.
_____ 17. Wands = creative energy.

_____ 18. Cups = feeling.
_____ 19. Swords = reality, tangibles.

Answers to Review of the Minor Arcana

MATCHING
1. **c**   2. **a**   3. **d**   4. **b**

TRUE OR FALSE
 1. **f**   2. **t**   3. **t**   4. **t**   5. **f**   6. **f**   7. **t**   8. **t**   9. **f** 10. **t**
11. **f** 12. **t** 13. **f** 14. **f** 15. **f** 16. **f** 17. **t** 18. **t** 19. **f**

THE MAJOR ARCANA INTRODUCED

In reviewing Lesson 1, we find that everyday life is depicted by the Minor Arcana. We encounter illustrations of the various aspects of life and personality traits of the people (the Court cards) who live our lives with us.

We see glory, competition and enterprises in the suit of Wands, and emotions, loved ones, friends and family in the suit of Cups. Sorrow, decisions, difficulties and attitudes are expressed in the Swords suit, and finances, reality, working and owning are shown in the Pentacles suit.

Have you noticed that something is missing? In looking over the various suits and their meaning, have you found some aspects of life unmentioned? Think about what is lacking.

If you guessed the psychic, psychological, philosophical and spiritual parts of life, you're correct. The Major Arcana of the Tarot, the cards you did not use in the previous lesson, represent these special, meaningful aspects. The 22 cards of the Major Arcana were the original Tarot, and have been more widely publicized than the Minor Arcana or Court cards. They are the trumps of the deck and the spiritual Tarot. Now place in front of you the 22 cards numbered 0 and 1-21 in Roman numerals: The Fool, The Magician, The High Priestess, The Empress, The Emperor, The Hierophant, The Lovers, The Chariot, Strength, The Hermit, Wheel of Fortune, Justice, The Hanged Man, Death, Temperance, The Devil, The Tower, The Star, The Moon, The Sun, Judgement and The World.

These cards show the spiritual significance of the lessons in life.

In addition, the cards are pictures, again symbolic, of the different parts of our psyche or spiritual, psychological makeup. The Magician, for example, symbolizes our conscious mind and ego. The High Priestess contains symbols of our subconscious mind. The Hierophant represents our intuitive faculties, while The Hermit suggests the principle of wisdom. All are innate factors within us, waiting to be awakened, focused and utilized.

When cards from the Major Arcana appear in a reading, major psychological and spiritual forces are at work in the question. Often a Major's appearance can suggest powerful energies entering the question that are somewhat beyond a person's complete control. The Major cards are rarely what they appear to be — their concepts and spiritual principles often remain hidden until probed. Death and The Devil, the most famous and notorious of the Tarot trumps, are good examples of this.

The Death trump, number XIII, has caused Tarot readers difficulty for many years. Individuals react terribly to its frightening image, when in reality the card is a harbinger of liberation and positive change! Of all the Major Arcana trumps, this one has been misused most severely by the uninformed media. On television and in the movies, we see a poor, unfortunate victim of a cartomancer having his or his loved one's demise predicted by the turn of the dreaded Death card. This makes Tarot scholars want to scream bloody murder at the misinformation created by inadequate research on the part of the screenwriter. The Death card does not represent a physical passing away but a transformation in life where the person has the opportunity to make a fresh start and create new conditions, more akin to rebirth of the new that requires the ending of the old and outworn. When you see the sun in The Death card, think sunrise, not sunset.

A while back I watched a movie that featured a sailor coming to port and having his fortune read by a haggard old lady. By the way, why are all Tarot readers characterized as witchlike, warty women? I for one am not fitting of that description, are you?

The sailor had the great misfortune of having The Hanged Man, who in an older version of Tarot employed in this particular movie was the "Drowned Man," appear as his Final Outcome.

I'm sure you can deduce the punch line to this saga: the sailor went back to his ship, fell overboard and was immediately drowned. Another point for the misrepresentation of Tarot!

The existence of The Devil card in the pack leads people to believe that the Tarot is the work of the Devil and those using this form of divination are in league with no other than Satan himself!

As we study The Devil trump, these delusions will be shed, but I must digress for a moment. The Tarot has had somewhat of a bad reputation in years past because of its use by black magicians, Satanists and witches for divination. These people employ the cards because of the powerful, correct readings the Tarot produces. Please remember, the Tarot may have been and may continue to be misused, but that does **not** indicate all Tarot readers are witches, black magicians or Satanists. I cannot emphasize this point enough. Tarot readers and students are generally very sane, intelligent people who simply sense that there is more to the universe than what their conscious mind and five senses tell them and they embark on discovering the potential of their inner selves, through symbolism that the Tarot very aptly provides.

Another inaccurate but basically entertaining and humorous presentation of the Tarot occurs in the James Bond movie, *Live and Let Die*. The Tarot cards are used by a beautiful priestess. Viewers see Mr. Bond stack the deck with nothing but The Lovers cards, thus ensuring the future of his romantic escapades!

Now choose two cards, one a favorite and one you dislike, from the Major Arcana. Compare these with your first choices in the Introduction. In choosing those first cards, you may have chosen Major Arcana cards. If you chose trumps, look up their meanings. Remember that the meanings apply to your inner thoughts or outer life at the time of the selection.

As you grow, your selections will change. This is a fascinating process to watch, especially for someone unfamiliar with the cards who continues to make selections based strictly on the cards' visual appeal. The cards chosen at different times do depict pertinent thoughts and needs within.

Each of the Major Arcana trumps has an astrological or planetary association attributed to it. You may discover new insights into your family, yourself, your talents and potentials by reviewing the appropriate Tarot trump associated with your birth sign:

Aries	The Emperor
Taurus	The Hierophant
Gemini	The Lovers
Cancer	The Chariot
Leo	Strength
Virgo	The Hermit
Libra	Justice

(continued on next page)

(continued from previous page)

Scorpio	Death
Sagittarius	Temperance
Capricorn	The Devil
Aquarius	The Star
Pisces	The Moon

The planets rule the remaining Tarot trumps, and studying those attributed to your sign may give you additional character information.

Mars	ruler of Aries	The Tower
Pluto	co-ruler of Scorpio with Mars	Judgement
Venus	Taurus and Libra	The Empress
Mercury	Gemini and Virgo	The Magician
The **Moon**	Cancer	The High Priestess
The **Sun**	Leo	The Sun
Jupiter	Sagittarius	Wheel of Fortune
Saturn	Capricorn	The World
Uranus	Aquarius	The Fool
Neptune	Pisces	The Hanged Man

The study of the Major Arcana is an ongoing, lifetime pursuit. These concepts are so vast that we can apply art, astrology, modern psychology, history, mythology, the Bible and Eastern and Western religions to the cards, thus producing an intensive, in-depth study.

The Major Arcana provide an unique, powerful link into meditation. Contemplating and integrating these concepts on an intuitional, spiritual level is truly a transforming practice for the initiate. The whole of the Self and one's discovery of the purpose on earth await the Tarot student who embarks on a supervised meditation program with a trained teacher.

In this introductory textbook, the Tarot is dealt with on a basic divinatory basis. Careful study and intuitive application of the description of each trump will inform you of some of the deep concepts the Tarot cards do truly embody. We will study much more about these especially fascinating cards of the Tarot later in this guide.

Review of the Major Arcana

TRUE OR FALSE

_____ 1. There are 21 cards in the Major Arcana.

_____ 2. The Major Arcana are the original Tarot cards, with the Minor Arcana added later through history.

_____ 3. "Trumps" is another term applied to the Major Arcana.

_____ 4. Everyday life and external events are represented by the Major Arcana.

_____ 5. There is no place in the Tarot to represent the spiritual, psychological aspects of life.

_____ 6. The inclusion of The Devil card indicates that the Tarot is controlled by Satan.

_____ 7. The appearance of the Death trump in a reading means that the person, or a close friend or relative, will soon die.

_____ 8. A majority of Major Arcana cards appearing in a reading indicates that the person is in complete control of the situation.

_____ 9. Each card from the Major Arcana is associated with a planet or sign of the zodiac.

_____ 10. Study of the Major Arcana can be an aid to meditation and spiritual growth.

_____ 11. The language of Tarot is a subconscious, symbolic language that we can use to interpret the future and recall the past.

_____ 12. We can choose Tarot cards without previous knowledge of their meanings and have them make sense in describing our lives because the subconscious recognizes and relates to these symbols.

Answers to Review of the Major Arcana

TRUE OR FALSE

1. f   2. t   3. t   4. f   5. f   6. f   7. f   8. f   9. t   10. t
11. t   12. t

PART II
READING DESCRIPTION

HOW TO START

This lesson presents eleven steps that take you through the process of a reading from beginning to end. It also includes some methods for further study to increase your growing knowledge of the Tarot.

First — Choosing the Question
The person who wants the reading thinks of one question to ask the cards. *Do not share it*

Second — Choosing the Indicator (Significator) Card
The Indicator card is chosen from the Court cards and the Major Arcana. Until you have studied the Major Arcana in Part III, confine your possible selections to the Court cards. The Indicator Card represents the person asking the question of the cards. That person is called the Seeker or Inquirer (Querent); the person performing the reading is the Reader.

If the Seeker is a woman over age 18, have her choose from the four Queens.

A male Seeker chooses an Indicator from the Knights and Kings. A man aged 18-35 is usually represented by a Knight. A man over age 35 is indicated by a King.

There are exceptions. Young men who are mature, responsible and settled may pick a King, while older men who are youthful, energetic and have many goals yet to reach may be attracted towards Knights. This is especially true if their question for the cards is about one of those goals.

If the Seeker is young, (birth to 18), he or she is to choose from the Pages. The Pages represent youths of either sex. An exceptionally mature 16, 17 or 18 year old may be more suited to having a Queen represent them if female or a Knight if male. In this case, go ahead and use the older Court cards.

Lay the appropriate Court cards in front of the Seeker. Have the Seeker choose the card he or she is drawn to. Make sure the Seeker concentrates on the one question being asked as the Indicator is selected.

After the Seeker has chosen an Indicator card, return the other Court cards to the deck and keep the Indicator card aside.

Third — Phrasing the Question *– Do not share it,*

Concentrate on the question chosen in the first step. The wording of the question is crucial to the success or failure of a reading, and must be carefully thought out. It should concern one topic, e.g., health, a relationship, moving, and so on, and be worded thusly: "What will happen with my _____ in the next _____ months?" For example, if the Seeker wants to know about job prospects for the next three months, he or she would ask the cards, "What will happen with my job prospects in the next three months?"

An alternative way to ask the question would be, "Show me my future concerning job prospects during the next three months." Either way of asking is acceptable if the question is clear, concise and specific. If the question is vague, without time limits or specification, the answer the cards give may be confusing.

Fourth — The Shuffle

The Seeker shuffles the deck, excluding the Indicator card, any way that he or she feels like handling the cards. The Seeker **must** concentrate on the question during the shuffling process, but keeps the question private. When the Seeker feels like stopping, the shuffling should stop.

The Seeker continues to keep the question private until during the reading, you the Reader inform the Seeker of the general area of the question, which the Seeker can then confirm. The reason for this is twofold: first, it requires more knowledge and concentration from you, the Reader, so you must approach the reading better equipped; and second, the Seeker will respect you more if you are able to tell what has been asked about. When I go to a Reader and am asked "What do you want to know about?" or "What are your questions?", I'm disappointed, because I think that the Reader should know at least something about why I'm there without my having to say. I tend to respect a Reader who can tune in to my topics of concern and tell me what I'm asking about. This is valid and makes the Seeker feel open and more trustful of the reading. As long as you are learning to read Tarot cards, you might as well learn to read the best way possible.

Fifth — Interpreting the Shuffle

The way the Seeker performs the shuffle can give you, the Reader, some special insights. Silently look for and note these clues:

Sloppy shuffling usually shows lack of concentration on the question, and leads to confusing readings. Remind the Seeker to think only about the question. Chances are his mind is wandering or he is talking to the Reader rather than silently concentrating

If the Seeker shuffles with the cards pointed away from you (assuming you, the Reader, are seated across from the Seeker) and toward himself, you are reading for a secretive, private person who may be shy about the question they have asked. This also applies if the cards are held close to the body and off the table. A person who shuffles in this way is skeptical, approaching the reading with reservations and doubt, and is likely to give you little information during the reading. Watch for other body language such as crossed arms and legs and moving the chair back from the table. The Seeker, closed and nonreceptive, is signaling you to tread lightly, not to delve too deeply. He may feel threatened by you or the question he is asking. Say nothing about this body language and try to respect the Seeker's privacy. You will be told when you've said enough.

On the other hand, an open person will point the cards toward you, or shuffle toward you, the message being, "Tell me everything you see!" S/he may reach across the table, placing the cards as close as possible to you and then lean forward, waiting for you to begin. This Seeker is eager to "know it all" and may have more of a conversation with you than a reading from you. S/he may hang on your every word and follow what you say too literally.

Both the open and the closed person may have unrealistic expectations about the reading you're giving. The enthusiastic Seeker may be disappointed when you can't tell every detail of the future, complete with names, dates and places! The nonreceptive or private Seeker may be so disbelieving or so frightened of what you have to say that s/he may block the reading. Often you may think you've done poorly with these individuals' readings only to hear from them a year later, at which time they enthusiastically tell you every detail of the reading and how it came true! It's hard to judge when you're doing a reading, as to whether or not you're hitting home. Time usually will tell, so don't judge yourself too hastily.

The balanced Seeker, one who knows his mind yet is open to your reading's viewpoint, is the most desirable to read for. This Seeker will shuffle on the middle of the table, somewhat toward himself. He will cut either from the middle to right, then left, or vice versa.

During the shuffling, cards may fall out or flip over accidentally. These are no accidents, though, and those cards' meanings can generally summarize the entire reading! Notice the cards that overturn or pop out while being shuffled. Remember whether they fall upright or reversed facing the Seeker. Don't be surprised if that same card appears in the reading or even flips out again before the shuffling is finished. This is highly significant, revealing an important influence in the reading. After noting the fallen cards, return them to the deck and have the Seeker continue shuffling.

Sixth — Reading the Cut
When the Seeker feels she's shuffled sufficiently, she stops. Ask her to cut the cards into three piles, face down. Traditionally, the left hand is used to make the Cut because it's the hand of the subconscious mind, and therefore revealing what the subconscious knows about the Seeker's question.

A Cut from left to right shows the Seeker's desire to know about the future. Conversely, if the Cut is made from right to left, the cards indicate patterns or concerns from the past.

When you read the Cut, the first pile down, or the pile that never left the table, is the Past. The second pile down is read as the Present. The third pile down is the Future. The piles are always read this way, regardless where the Seeker places them on the table.

Seventh — Interpreting the Cut
A Cut starting from the middle, going to one side of the middle pile, and then the other side is balanced. This is a horizontal cut meaning openness with good personal judgment.

A horizontal Cut, from left to right reveals that hidden, unexpected or unconscious motivations and information may come to light when the Cut is read. Sometimes this information is about the Seeker's future.

Conversely, if the Cut is made from right to left, the Seeker is searching or asking the subconscious for guidance and information about the question. The Seeker who cuts this way may be asking why or what has caused the situation to occur.

If the Seeker is left-handed, this theory operates in reverse.

Turn over the three piles, making sure you turn them as you would a page in a book rather than from top to bottom. (Turn over the entire pile, not the first or top card.) Turning the cards over from right to left ensures that they face the Seeker, not the Reader, the way the Seeker dealt them. This is assuming that you are seated opposite each other. The psychic energies flow better if you sit on opposite sides of a desk or table.

Let's use an illustration to make these points clear. The Seeker has finished shuffling and has cut the cards, starting from the center and going from one side to the other of the central pile. Pile number 1 is the Past, because it never left the table or was the first pile placed on the table if the Seeker was holding the entire deck during the cutting process. Let's assume the Reader and the Seeker are seated opposite each other; the card titled Three of Wands is reversed when we turn pile number one over, facing the Seeker. This is read as the Past and with the reversed meaning of the Three of Wands.

The second pile placed on the table has the Queen of Cups facing toward the Seeker. This is the Seeker's Present. The Queen of Cups is read upright.

The third pile is always the last pile to be placed on the table regardless where the Seeker places it. The card is Temperance upright (facing the Seeker).

Fig. 1

READER SEATED HERE

Pile 2	Pile 1	Pile 3
Queen of Cups	3 of Wands	Temperence
PRESENT	Reversed	**FUTURE**
	PAST	
Presently, you're sensitive and emotional about your question. Make sure you're using reason and common sense rather than letting your imagination run away with you.	In your **past,** concerning the topic of your question, you experienced lack of cooperation and disappointment in others. Your energies were scattered and disorganized.	There will be a possibility of new adjustments and adaptation in the **future.** A new balance to look forward to. Future good management.

SEEKER SEATED HERE

The next step is to TURN THE THREE PILES OVER (FACE DOWN) AND HAVE THE SEEKER PUT THEM INTO ONE PILE ANY WAY DESIRED.

Pile 3 last pile

Watch carefully as the Seeker puts the cards back together into one pile. If the Future pile ends up on top, the reading will basically deal with what is to come. When the Present pile is placed on top, the Seeker's reading will emphasize dealing with present situations. Placing the Past pile on top indicates that the reading will be about past situations that may have to be dealt with i.e., repeated cycles (possibly mistakes); or the reading may shed light on how situations were previously handled and how to change and/or utilize this information.

The Cut can also be interpreted using body language. The private person will cut away from you towards himself. The open person cuts toward the Reader and away from himself. We can interpret this the same as we would the private or open Seeker's shuffling.

You, the Reader, then take the deck and **turn it to face you** so that you can look at the Reading the way it fell in front of the Seeker.

Again, the deck must be switched to face the Reader so you can lay the reading out facing yourself. If you and your friend were reading this book and one of you were sitting across from the other, you would have to turn the book around so your friend could read it. The same idea applies to turning the cards: you have to turn them to read them as they fell for the Seeker.

This is such an important point that I'd like to explain it another way. With the shuffling, cutting and putting back together complete, you have the deck sitting in front of you as the Seeker has left it. Turn the very first card over, right to left, and notice whether it is reversed or upright facing the Seeker. This is your key; if it is upright, then you have to get the deck to face you keeping the first card upright, because that is the way the cards have fallen for the Seeker. The only way to do this is to turn the deck around. By remembering to turn the deck to face you before each reading, you can eliminate this step of turning over the first card.

Keep in mind two rules:

1. Always open the cards like a book, from left to right or vice versa, never top to bottom.
2. Always turn the entire deck to face you just before you begin your reading, exception if you and the Seeker are sitting side by side.

Fig.2

READER SITS HERE

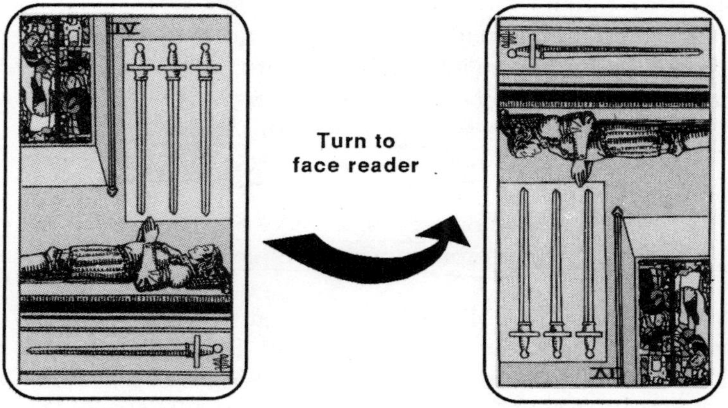

Turn to
face reader

1. Original way cards are faced.
FACES SEEKER

2. Cards now face Reader.
READING CAN BEGIN.

SEEKER SITS HERE

Eighth — Interpreting the Indicator

Turn the Indicator card to face you, the Reader. The Indicator card shows what the Seeker wants to know about or how he or she is approaching the question.

First, note the suit of the Court card. If the suit of Wands was chosen, then the question may be ambitious in nature. Perhaps the Seeker is asking about an idea or enterprise that he would like to initiate or has put a great deal of energy into. Maybe there are strong desires connected to the question, or maybe the Seeker is energetic, creative and courageous, using qualities of leadership and enthusiasm. The astrological sun sign of the Seeker has little bearing when it comes to choosing an Indicator card. The choice of Wands always indicates strong desires wrapped up in the matter. Goals and desires are the terms on which Wands people approach the question.

If a Cups Court card was chosen, the Seeker may be emotional and sensitive about the matter. Family, loved ones and intuitive feelings are the terms on which Cups people approach the question.

If a Swords Court card was selected, the matter may have decision-making, aggression or some strife connected with it. Cutting away from the past, separating positive from negative and serious thinking may be topics of concern. Action and intelligence are the terms on which Swords people approach the question.

Pentacles are chosen when personal or financial security, jobs, property and money are the areas in question. Realistic, practical matters and material matters may be the question's topic.

The choice of a Pentacles Indicator card means that the Seeker approaches the question in terms of realism and practicality. Sometimes the Indicator can represent what the Seeker is trying to use as far as qualities of character are concerned, e.g., a desire to understand how a situation really stands.

From this information we can observe how the Seeker is looking at the question and sometimes the topic of the question itself.

Ninth — Placement Meanings (see Figure 3.)
Placement refers to the design, or spread, in which the cards are laid out. The spread used in the *Easy Tarot Guide* is called the Celtic cross. It has been given this name because of its resemblance to the actual Celtic cross, which has a circle around the intersection of the crossbar and shaft. In this 10-card Tarot spread, the first two cards form a cross, with the next four cards forming a circle around them. The two cards represent the core or heart of the matter now at hand. The four cards encircling them provide insight into the past and the future of the question. Of the four remaining cards, the next three offer additional information about the less visible, more internal circumstances surrounding the question; the final card speaks to the outcome — or final answer — of the question within the limits set by the Seeker.

There are other traditional Tarot spreads, but the Celtic Cross is the oldest and most popular. It also provides the most-in-depth information for a reading.

The card placements are numbered from 1 to 10, indicating the order in which the cards are laid down and then interpreted. Each placement has a specific meaning that you combine with the card's meaning when you give the interpretation.

Placement 1. The first placement represents the Present conditions surrounding the Seeker's question. It shows what is going on now.
Placement 2. The second placement represents either the Helping Force (for a positive card) or Obstacles or Problems (if a negative card). This card is laid sideways across the first. It is always read upright (right side up).

Placement 3. The third placement describes the Seeker's Past experience concerning that matter. It also shows why he has asked the question today, based on his past experience. This card is placed below cards 1 and 2. (See Figure 3.)

Placement 4. The fourth placement describes the Recent Past, the influences just passing out of the Seeker's situation, again in reference to the question asked. It is laid to the immediate left of cards 1 and 2.

Placement 5. The fifth placement shows the Possible Future. This interpretation is a flexible one; sometimes it is the future as the Seeker sees it now. This card can also represent an alternative future, or what could *possibly* happen from today's standpoint.

Placement 6. The sixth placement is important because it is the Immediate Future card. This card tells what will happen next concerning the question asked.

Placement 7. The seventh placement indicates the Seeker's Attitude toward the question. It is his other viewpoint, showing how the Seeker is thinking about the question right now.

Placement 8. The eighth placement is the Seeker's Environment (also called Other's Viewpoint). It tells what is happening in the environment of the question (e.g., home, work) or it describes the opinion and viewpoint of family and friends — those in the Seeker's environment — about the issue in question.

Placement 9. The ninth placement deals with the Hopes and Fears of the Seeker. If the card is positive, it shows the Seeker's hopes; if negative, the Seeker's fears. It does not necessarily show how things will work out.

Placement 10. The tenth placement is the Final Outcome. This card indicates how the question will be resolved or what will happen within the time reference specified in the question. The Reader can look to Placement 5, the Possible Future, for confirmation or denial of the statement of the tenth card.

Celtic Cross

Fig. 3

5

Possible Future

10

Final
Outcome

9

Hopes &
Fears

Present Influence

1

2

4

Recent Event
(a couple of
months)

Helps & Hindrances
Present

6

Immediate
Future

8

1.Environment
--home or work
2.How others
see you in the
situation

3

Past

7

On your mind
Mental Outlook
How you see it

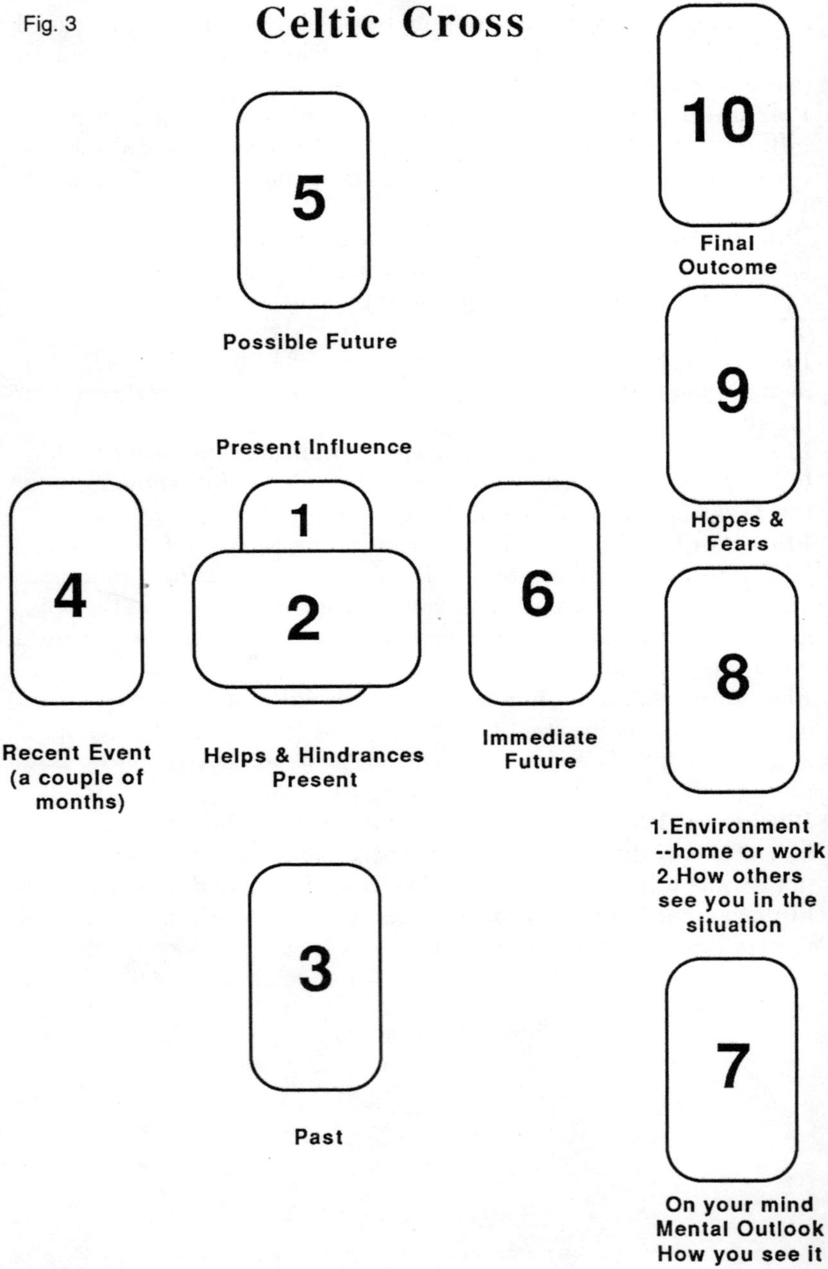

Lay out the following reading:

THE INDICATOR
Indicator card — Knight of Wands

THE READING
Placement 1   Present Influence — Four of Swords
Placement 2   Helps or Obstacles — Seven of Swords
Placement 3   Past, Motivation — The Devil reversed
Placement 4   Recent Past — Justice
Placement 5   Possible Future — Three of Pentacles
Placement 6   Immediate Future — Queen of Swords
Placement 7   Seeker's Attitude — Temperance
Placement 8   Seeker's Environment/Others' Viewpoint — Five of
                 Wands
Placement 9   Hopes and Fears — The Hanged Man reversed
Placement 10.   Final Outcome — Ace of Swords

An Interpretation of this Reading

1. When you turn the first card over, say, "This is your present situation concerning the question asked."
   The Four of Swords has come up for the Present card. Look up the meaning in the interpretation section. Here is how we put the Placement — in this case the Present — and the card's meaning together: "At present, you are temporarily resting or having a truce from a difficult situation. You know the problem is not over yet; you are just retreating for the time being." (This is the meaning of the Four of Swords.)

2. In looking up the Seven of Swords you find that this is a negative card. The meaning is theft, unfairness and being used, so these forces would now be hindering the Seeker. You can interpret this for the Seeker by saying, "At present, you have unfairness and betrayal causing obstacles or going against you in your situation."

3. You can see from the interpretations that the Devil reversed means that in the past the Seeker has had the willpower to overcome the selfish, manipulative tendencies in his nature when dealing with the question asked.

4. In the layout, the Justice trump of the Major Arcana fell upright. Recently, therefore, the Seeker has felt an urge for growth and change toward developing personal goals. There has been new balance in his life. He has been receiving what he deserves.

5. The Three of Pentacles is the Possible Future card. We will interpret it as possible achievement of mastery over the question asked. Notice this is only possible, not definite, because of the card's placement.

Q Swords

6. A woman who is strong-minded and decisive in nature will influence the Seeker in perhaps a counseling or advisory way. Her judgment will be insightful and perceptive; her viewpoint will be reliable. She may guide him in a decision-making process. The Seeker may have a conversation with this woman. This is an important card because it tells us what will happen next.

7. Temperance is the attitude card, indicating that the Seeker's Attitude is one of cooperation and adaptation.

8. With the Five of Wands, friends and family see the Seeker in stressful, strife-ridden conditions. Or you can interpret this card as fighting and competition going on in the work or home environment. Ask the Seeker which interpretation is correct.

9. The Hanged Man reversed is a negative card, indicating the Seeker's fears are of his own selfishness and pride. Remember that he overcame them in the past. See Placement three.

10. The tenth card is the Ace of Swords. There will be a victory through use of willpower, mind over matter. Obstacles will be overcome, in which case the answer would be yes. You can look to the Possible Future, Placement five, for confirmation of this or contradiction — in this reading, you see the Three of Pentacles, so there is a confirmation of mastery or victory over circumstances.

Tenth — Make General Observations

Besides analyzing the placement of the cards, the Reader should also be alert to larger patterns that appear in the spread. By observing these patterns and how they relate to the placements, the Reader can pick up additional information about the theme of the reading, the progress of the issue, and other circumstances surrounding the Seeker. To obtain this additional information, the Reader uses the techniques of suit assessment and card counting, and also notes the occurrence of significant card combinations.

SUIT ASSESSMENT

Look for a central theme signified by a predominance of certain cards.

Predominant Major Arcana. When there are more Major Arcana cards in a layout than a dominant suit, the situation pertains to a considerably momentous matter. A predominance of cards from the Major Arcana indicates that the Seeker's question may be extremely significant and powerful. The hand of *Destiny* may be controlling the matter rather than the Seeker.

Dominant Reversed. Eight or more cards appearing reversed indicate either that the Seeker is upset about the question or that the question itself is of a distressing nature.

If all ten cards are reversed, the reading should be **reshuffled**, including the Cut, and cast again. Remember to formulate the question correctly, i.e., "What will happen in the future with _____?" Ensure that full concentration is present during the shuffling and question-forming procedure. Check that all the cards in the deck aren't facing the same direction. If the second attempt produces all inverted cards, the reading should be cast at another time.

Predominant Court Cards. These can be others involved in and influencing the question. The Court cards may also represent different aspects of the Seeker's personality expressed in relation to the question. That is, they show how the Seeker or other people involved in the inquiry may behave.

Predominant Suit.

(a) If Wands are predominant, the question is about a matter that the Seeker feels ambitious toward. He regards the situation as an enterprise, adventure or challenge.

(b) If there is a predominance of Cups, the Seeker is emotional and sensitive about the question being asked. The question itself may be about an emotional matter.

(c) If the Swords suit is predominant, the Seeker questions what action will be taken by himself or others concerning the topic. The inquiry may concern a battle of some sort, or the Seeker may regard the situation as a type of war. Thinking, strife, worrying, questioning and debating are the mental struggles that may be occurring when the Seeker has predominance of Swords cards.

(d) When the Pentacles dominate, the Seeker is approaching the matter with a practical attitude, or is desirous of being realistic. The question may deal with finances, property or job and economic matters.

CARD COUNTING (NUMBER TREND)

Determine the number trend by adding the numbers of the cards from both Minor and Major Arcana in the Celtic layout. Then reduce the number to one digit by adding the double digit together, with the exception of numbers 11 and 22. The Court Cards are not considered since they are not numbered.

Example: 27 becomes 2 + 7 = 9; 32 becomes 3 + 2 = 5; 85 becomes 8 + 5 = 13 and this becomes 1 + 3 = 4; 83 becomes 8 + 3 = 11 and remains 11. The final number or reduced digit is the General Theme of the Reading.

Note: If a reading adds up to 10 or if 10's dominate in a reading, interpret this as the ending of a cycle with the initiation of a new one.

INTERPRETATION OF NUMBERS
One (1): Beginnings, initiation, change, starting something new.
Two (2): Relating to others, partnership, communication, sharing, weighing or balancing alternatives and opportunities.
Three (3): Growth, multiplying, plans beginning to become real.
Four (4): Stablization, security, materialization, reality, situation is established.
Five (5): Change, disruption, growth-producing but difficult because the changes are not desired. Upset circumstances, disharmony.
Six (6): Harmony restored, balance, sharing, security.
Seven (7): Success, retreat, a soul number. Victory concerning ideals or personal ambitions, soul unfoldment.
Eight (8): Success, financially or with power issues; control, dominion, balanced expression of power. Healing power.
Nine (9): Achievement, more on a personal level concerning goals, ideals, emotional, mental or spiritual matters. Attainment and endings.
Ten (10): Ending of one cycle and beginning of a new one.
Eleven (11): Spiritual, psychic, artistic, innovative, original, creative matters.
Twenty-Two (22): Money or powerful wealth, spiritual mastery.

SIGNIFICANCE OF PREVAILING NUMBERS
OF THE MINOR ARCANA
Observe the prevailing numbers. Note whether they are mostly beginning numbers: Aces, Twos and Threes. Middle and development numbers are Fours, Fives, Sixes and Sevens. Ending or conclusion numbers are Eights, Nines and Tens.

If most of the numbers are low — Aces, Twos and Threes — the Seeker's question deals with a matter in its early or starting stages.

If the middle numbers — Fours, Fives, Sixes and Sevens — prevail, the Seeker's situation is already established or ongoing. The question is in the midway stage.

If the higher numbers — Eights, Nines and Tens — are strongest, the Seeker is reaching the end or the conclusion stage of the matter.

CARD COMBINATIONS

When a reading contains certain similar cards, the general theme of the reading is strengthened or confirmed. The following are the themes for certain combinations of cards appearing in a reading:

1. Violence — Strength reversed; Ace of Swords reversed; King of Wands, Cups or Swords reversed; Queen of Wands reversed; Knight of Wands reversed; Knight of Swords reversed; Eight of Wands reversed and The Tower card.
2. Infidelity — Three of Cups reversed; The Lovers reversed; The Empress reversed; Queen of Wands reversed; two Knights, Kings or Queens in a romantic reading; The Moon (deception); The Tower and Page of Swords (secrets are exposed).
3. Good decisions or choices — The Fool; The Lovers; Two of Swords reversed; Seven of Cups reversed.
4. Wrong choices — The Fool reversed; The Lovers reversed; The Devil.
5. (a) Lawsuits, fair outcome — Justice; King or Queen of Swords upright; Ace of Swords; The Chariot; The World; Six of Pentacles; Six of Wands.
   (b) Lawsuits, unfair outcome — King or Queen of Swords reversed; Knight of Swords reversed; Justice reversed; Ace of Swords reversed; Ten of Swords or Wands; Six of Pentacles reversed; Six of Wands reversed. A lawyer is represented by the King of Cups; King of Swords; Queen of Swords or The Magician. The Hermit represents legal advice.
6. Marriage — The Lovers; Ten of Cups; The Empress; Four of Wands; Three of Cups for engagements; The Sun. The Hierophant represents traditional legal or orthodox marriage.
   Note: The Hierophant reversed is common-law marriage or an unusual, original marital agreement.
7. (a) Health — Good, overcoming difficulties — The Sun; The Lovers; The Star; The Chariot; Strength; The World; Judgement; Justice (balance); The Empress; Temperance (balance); Ace of Swords, Cups, Wands and Pentacles; Three of Pentacles; Four of Wands; Wheel of Fortune.

(b) Medical advice — The Hermit; King and Queen of Swords; The Magician, King of Cups. The Hermit upright is following medical advice; reversed, is ignoring medical advice. The Magician or the Queen and King of Swords may be medical specialists or advisers. The King of Cups may be a kind doctor counseling the Seeker.

(c) Mental and emotional health problems — The Empress reversed; The Lovers reversed; The Chariot reversed; Strength reversed; Queen of Cups and Pentacles reversed.

(d) Eyesight problems — The Emperor or The Sun reversed.

(e) Ulcer or stomach problems — The Chariot reversed.

(f) Heart, back or spinal problems — Strength reversed; Ten of Wands upright or reversed.

(g) Dietary imbalance — The Chariot reversed.

(h) Dietary, nutritional and general health advice — The Hermit.

(i) Overcoming health problems through controlling habits — The Chariot; Strength upright.

(j) Health problems recur from the past — Wheel of Fortune reversed; Nine of Wands upright and reversed.

(k) Resistance to disease, guarding one's health with alertness to symptoms, preserved health through carefulness — Nine of Wands. Reversed, health problems recur, the Seeker isn't bothering to maintain his health.

(l) Medical tests passed — Temperance upright.

(m) Medical tests failed — Temperance reversed.

(n) Recuperation, hospitalization, vacation for health reasons — Four of Swords.

(o) Breakdowns may be indicated by The Tower.

(p) Depression and anxiety — Nine of Swords; The Sun and The Star reversed and Five of Pentacles.

(q) Psychological counseling — Strength card.

(r) Poor health, a health failure of some sort, organic or system malfunction — The Sun reversed.

(s) Poor or no healing, health imbalance, breathing or lung problems — The Lovers reversed.

(t) Surgery to eliminate difficulties — Three of Swords. Minor surgery is the Three of Swords reversed.

(u) Internal or organic malfunctions — Seven of Pentacles both upright and reversed.

(v) Muscular or skeletal difficulties, problems with limbs — Ten of Wands.

8. Unhappy endings or failure — Three of Swords; Ten of Wands; Ten of Swords; Eight of Cups; Five of Cups.
9. Happy endings — Three of Cups; Ace of Swords; Ten of Cups; The Sun; The World; Judgement; Four of Wands; Six of Swords; Eight of Wands; Three of Pentacles; Six of Wands; The Chariot.

Review of Observations and Layout

Use the layout that you spread from the ninth section, "Placement Meanings," to answer the questions that follow.

MAKE YOUR OBSERVATIONS

1. Indicator card
   a. Suit _____
   b. Meaning _____

2. Character interpretation _____

3. a. Major Suit _____
   (Highest amount of cards of one suit, Court cards or Major Arcana)
   b. Second Major Suit _____
   The second Major suit is the suit with the equal amount or second highest amount of cards in the reading.)

4. Reversed cards
   Amount _____

5 a. Number trend _____
   b. Meaning _____

6. The Seeker fears his selfishness and pride as shown by the _____ card. Placement number _____.
   Placement meaning _____.

7. The Seeker has recently taken action toward new balance and fairness in his dealings. The card showing this is _____. Placement number _____.
   Placement meaning _____.

8. In the past the Seeker let go of his fears and learned a lesson about being manipulative and powerful. Card _____. Placement number _____.
   Placement meaning _____.

9. He has an adaptable, cooperative attitude as seen in the card _____. Placement number _____.
   Placement meaning _____.

10. Remember the Swords symbolism of the double-edge? It represents the concept of positive and negative and the mind's thinking. How the Seeker views his dilemma or the attitude he takes would therefore be significant.
   Why? _____.

11. There is a woman influencing the matter in a constructive, decisive way. Who is she? _____.
   When will she make her appearance? _____.
12. Compare the Possible Future and Final Outcome

   _____.

13. The people in the environment of the question may be causing the Seeker strife and competition. We see this in the _____ card. Placement number _____.
   Placement meaning _____.
14. The Seeker is presently retreating to contemplate a matter that is opposing him. This matter concerns retaliation and revenge and how he deals with it. What two cards show this? _____, _____.
   Placement numbers _____ and _____.
   These placements mean _____
   and _____.
15. Will his character help him deal with the situation? _____
   How? _____

Answers to Review of Observations and Layout

1. a. Wands
    b. ambitious, energetic, courageous, enthusiastic or any of the other meanings we take for the suit of Wands.
2. (See notes on Knight of Wands). A young man may be courageous and determined to handle situation in a valorous manner.
3. a. Swords-4
    b. Major Arcana-4
4. 2
5. a. Middle of situation because of dominant 4, 5 and 7.
    b. Seeker is in the middle of his dilemma.
6. The Hanged Man reversed, 9, Hopes and Fears
7. Justice, 4, Recent Past
8. The Devil reversed, 3, Past, Motivation
9. Temperance, 7, Attitude or how Seeker views the question.
10. The strong Sword suit indicates his outlook can help or hurt him. It could even affect his actions and the reading's outcome.
11. Queen of Swords, Immediate Future. This may be the next turn of events regarding his question.
12. They are the same; victory in 10th, mastery in 3rd.
13. Five of Wands and other people and their viewpoints, or how they affect the Seeker. Placement #8. Environment.
14. Four of Swords, Seven of Swords; 1 and 2; Present influence, Helps and Obstacles.
15. Yes. He is using courage, energy and optimism because he chose the suit of Wands.

Eleventh — The Diary
Serious Tarot scholars should keep a diary or notebook where they record readings along with the results. Often students come to me about a reading they've performed and draw a blank when they try to remember all the cards and where they fell. It is wise, early in Tarot work, to keep a record of readings for reference. Much insight about how the cards work and communicate can be determined through this procedure.

Hindsight is an excellent teacher if we take the time to learn from its lessons. When looking back to compare the outcome of a Tarot reading to how the cards fell, I usually observe that their message concerning the Future was quite correct and clear, though of course it may have been misinterpreted at the time.

EXAMPLE OF DIARY FORMAT

Reading cast for _____ **Date** _____
Question _____

The Cut
Past _____ Int. _____
Present _____ Int. _____
Future _____ Int. _____
Indicator _____ Int. _____

General Observations
Number Upright_____Number Reversed_____
Predominant   Theme_____
Int. _____
Secondary   Theme_____
Int. _____
Numerical   Grouping_____
Int. _____
Number of Reading_____
Int. _____
Summary _____
Card 1_____   Int._____
_____
Card 2_____   Int._____
_____
Card 3_____   Int._____
_____
Card 4_____   Int._____
_____
Card 5_____   Int._____
_____
Card 6_____   Int._____
_____
Card 7_____   Int._____
_____

(continued on next page)

Card 8_____   Int._____
_____
Card 9_____   Int._____
_____
Card 10_____   Int._____
_____
Summary _____
_____

FILLING IN THE DIARY

The Diary will help you acquire the habit of recording your readings and correctly analyzing the observations to fully benefit from the reading's content.

1. The name, date and question are self-explanatory. Astrologers may want to include the time the reading was performed on the date line.
2. Record the Cut cards. A basic phrase or key words may be jotted down.
3. Record the Indicator card with its accompanying interpretation.
4. Insert the names of the cards that fell in the spaces provided on the chart.

Record general observations before the reading begins. The abbreviation "Int." stands for the word interpretation. The Number Upright and Reversed refers to the total number of cards that appear upright or reversed in the spread, not including the Cut. When more than eight cards fall reversed, the Seeker may be upset and is inquiring about a personal difficulty.

The Dominant Theme of the reading is determined by observing the layout and discovering whether most of the cards belong to a suit, the Court or the Major Arcana. The Secondary Theme is determined from the second highest number of cards belonging to one suit, the Court or the Major Arcana.

Remember the main theme of the suits: Wands — ambitions, enterprises, goals and desires; Cups — emotions or feelings, intuition, family, loved ones; Swords — thoughts, actions, reactions, battles and decisions; Pentacles — materialism, work, possessions and reality.

A predominance of Court cards suggests that either: many people are involved with the inquiry; or the Seeker is experiencing an identity crisis or awareness. (Note: Pages may not necessarily be people, but personality and events or messages.)

Analyzing the numerical grouping requires observing whether the main numbers of the Minor Arcana in the reading are low (Aces, Twos and Threes), indicating the beginning of a matter; middle (Fours, Fives, Sixes and Sevens), suggesting the middle or developmental stages of a situation; or high (Eights, Nines and Tens), suggesting the conclusion of a situation.

The Reading Number refers to the numerology of the layout. Using the Placements 1 through 10 and disregarding the Cut, add all the numbers, remembering to count Aces as One. The Majors are numbered also, but the Court cards are not. When you reach the total number, add the digits together until a final, single digit is reached. If, when you add the digits, you arrive at 11 or 22, the number remains. Refer to section "Card Counting" under "Make General Observations" for further interpretation.

Your summary will bring the general observations together into a few key words or phrases that will guide your interpretation of the reading.

PART III
CARD INTERPRETATIONS

ACES, TWOS AND THREES

The Aces

Place the four Aces on a table in front of you. (Always look at your cards when you are working on them.)

The Aces are the most powerful cards of the Minor Arcana and carry important significance in a reading. These cards contain the root force of the suit's ruling astrological element (fire — Wands, water — Cups, air — Swords and earth — Pentacles) in their pictures.

The element of fire and its active, combustible force can be felt from the Ace of Wands. Fire is symbolic of our desires toward ambitions and goals in our life. Water in the Ace of Cups, with its flowing, creative and spiritual aspects, personifies our feeling nature with which we also flow. Power, mental and aggressive, exudes from the Ace of Swords in the air suit, suggesting this card's element as active and positively expressed. Air symbolizes the wind, always moving and changing, a perfect metaphor for our thoughts and actions in life.

The force of earth, its stability and solidity, is clearly felt from the Ace of Pentacles. Notice in this Ace that the garden has been cultivated and tended, suggesting to us that skill, forethought, effort and perseverance are qualities needed to make our dreams tangible and real.

The Ace of Wands represents our ideas and ambitions; the Ace of Cups is our dreams and imagination; the Ace of Swords, our thinking and organizing actions; the Ace of Pentacles stands for the actual materialized result.

All four Aces have symbolism that expresses the idea of the Creative Principle, just as Michaelangelo depicted it in the Sistine Chapel when he painted God creating Adam. The two figures are joined together by the touch of the fingertips of their open hands. The open hand is a representation of our Creator; the cloud suggests the mysteries involved in Creation. In the Tarot, this Creative Principle is portrayed in the Aces, the birth of the four suits. Reversed Aces have selfishness involved with the powerful energies.

ACE OF WANDS

The Ace of Wands represents the beginning of an idea, enterprise, ambition, desire or goal. Interpret this as the beginning of a situation where the Seeker feels a natural sense of enthusiasm, initiative, energy and courage.

Reversed — The new venture or goal may experience difficulties and delays. The Seeker should be careful of being selfish, demanding or unyielding.

ACE OF CUPS

The Ace of Cups is also a beginning, but this time of an emotional matter. Emotional growth, a new love or a new way of loving in an understanding way takes place. Understanding of self, receiving understanding, or giving understanding are the main interpretations of this Ace. In the Ace of Cups the water in the card is flowing, suggesting an outpouring of the emotional, feeling nature.

The white dove brings an initiation into the spiritual love that is our source — love expressed with kindness and compassion.

Reversed — When this card falls reversed, the Seeker cannot flow with his or her feelings or may be selfish with the giving and receiving of love (e.g., conditional love, manipulating loved ones, rejecting and playing games with others' feelings.

ACE OF SWORDS

The Ace of Swords suggests power; you can sense strength and will from the card. The mountains in the background indicate obstacles and difficulties that must be dealt with. The symbolism of the crown tells us that these problems have been or are beginning to be surmounted and conquered. Because it is the suit of the mind, the Seeker is required to use mental strength, willpower and determination. The victory is to be achieved by applying mind over matter and discipline. The Seeker is not using brutal or forceful tactics to accomplish his mission, but a balance of honest and ethical actions and motivations; peace and justice are the desired result. These facts are symbolized by the palm of triumph, coupled with the olive branch of armistice that we see hanging from the crown of conquest in the card.

Reversed — This card can be negative. Turn the card reversed. See how the sword seems to be plunging downward rather threateningly? This is how the Seeker is faring when this card appears inverted in a reading. He may feel threatened, pressured, victimized and beset with insurmountable problems. The Seeker may be the one causing these conditions.

ACE OF PENTACLES

The Ace of Pentacles is the suit of earth, indicating practical, concrete or physical matters. This Ace depicts a cultivated garden, suggesting knowledge and patience will produce fruits for our labors. This beginning is a visible, tangible one, often having to do with job, business, property matters, new work, prosperity, stability or purchases. A situation will manifest with real results.

Reversed — The situation the Seeker is asking about will not come to pass, or he or she may be finding dissatisfactory circumstances within job, money or business efforts. There are losses in general concerning Pentacle matters.

The Twos

Now place the four Twos on the table. The concept of balance is the basic theme of the Twos.

TWO OF WANDS

In the Two of Wands we see the balance of previous success (the wand fastened behind the merchant indicates prior accomplishments behind him or in his past) with ideas about a purposeful new enterprise. The merchant is looking toward the future with deep sincerity and belief or faith in his new ambition. The balance of the white lilies, symbolizing good intentions with red roses of devotion, suggests sincerity toward his goal. He holds a new wand, symbolizing his new enterprise, in one hand; in the other he has the globe of potential or dominion. His goal has deep meaning for him and he feels "meant" to pursue this new desire as if it were part of his personal fulfillment. He is balancing his idea, the wand, with its potential, the globe. This stage deals just with ideas that he has put out to see what will return in the form of feedback, acceptance, encouragement or confirmation. In this card, we see him waiting for results, concerning a job prospect, admittance to a school, prospective investors or an answer in general.

Reversed — This card still indicates ideas with sincerity, but the potentials may not be realized or results may not work out. There is disillusionment as little or nothing happens in regard to the desired goal.

TWO OF CUPS

Balance is indicated in a number of ways in the Two of Cups. This is a picture of a sharing relationship, friendship, partnership or romance where the mind and emotions are balanced. This card can indicate a discussion of importance between friends, lovers, partners or family members, mutual exchange of sharing and caring within a friendship or romance. We achieve this integration by making sure that loving balances with friendship and intellectual sharing.

A reciprocal give-and-take is pictured. Passion balanced with spirituality is the symbolism of the Lion and the Caduceus. Magnetic attraction between a couple is also indicated.

Reversed — Arguments and serious disagreements occur. Romantically, the infatuation wears off; resentments and hatred could result. Loss of balance leads to emotionalism, selfishness and rejection of a friend or lover. The relationship has lost its balance. Someone may be doing all the giving while the other is doing all the taking.

TWO OF SWORDS

We see emotions in the Two of Swords also. They are symbolized by the water in the background of the card. Notice the woman in the card turns her back on her emotions; her blindfold tells us that she cannot see clearly, and her position suggests the action of waiting the situation out, being passive. Occasionally in the Swords suit we see inaction rather than action. Because of her need for emotional balance, the woman has postponed, for the time being, facing truths and emotional facts. The Seeker, desiring harmony, decides not to decide for the time being. A decision is postponed so the Seeker can regain emotional balance. Unable to make a decision, the Seeker remains in the same situation, but eventually a decision will have to be made.

Reversed — The decision is made; action concerning a choice occurs. Sometimes the Seeker makes the decision; often it is made for the Seeker by circumstances. Look to future cards to reveal whether the decision is beneficial.

TWO OF PENTACLES

The Infinity symbol surrounds the two pentacles (coins) in the Two of Pentacles card. This symbol implies that change is infinite and that we must always expect fluctuation when dealing with what we own and possess, including loved ones, jobs and positions in life. We evolve from child to parent, dependent to independent and sometimes back to dependent again. The Infinity symbol tells us this principle of change is eternal and somewhat out of our hands, and that we can flow with these moves and rearrangements in life. The character in the card balances the pentacles easily, showing that flexibility and adaptability can help us accept change. Change in our daily life is eternal and always taking place. Here the Seeker grasps this fact and expects to flow with change. This can manifest as the ability to be flexible, to work two jobs; to consider new ventures while continuing to handle present ones, to juggle money to pay bills and to handle various, numerous responsibilities between the professional and personal life. New ventures have rough starts.

Reversed — The juggler drops the pentacles. Perhaps he is not going with his life's changing flow or is mishandling money or practical matters. The Seeker may be unable to handle commitments, biting off more than can be chewed, spending carelessly, spreading himself too thin financially or robbing Peter to pay Paul. Unexpected complications require the Seeker's adjustment. The Seeker encounters discouragement, inflexibility, difficulty in flowing with changes. Opposing factors within a situation seem impossible to remedy.

The Threes

The main theme of the Threes is growth.

THREE OF WANDS

We can see growth in the Three of Wands card quite easily because the ships are returning home, indicating development of a venture. Growth has occurred concerning the ideas that were put out; results are now forthcoming. This card indicates growth, positive results, success, cooperative efforts, teamwork and helpful advice.

Reversed — An admired person falls from the pedestal that the Seeker put him or her on. Enterprises do not grow. Spreading oneself too thin, lack of cooperation and poor teamwork plague the Seeker.

THREE OF CUPS

The Three of Cups depicts a relationship growing and developing. Giving and receiving have brought expansion. We see the characters in the Three of Cups celebrating the joy of love alliances, family or friendship. This card means happy results, growth in love, or finding someone with whom to build a lasting relationship. Another meaning is planning for love's future through an engagement, weddings or promises. Successful endings indicate the celebration of graduations, promotions, restored health (recovery), births, anniversaries and employment. The family and friends gather. The Seeker experiences positive and rewarding expression of natural abilities and creativity.

Reversed — An unhappy ending. The relationship doesn't grow. It can be spoiled by too much of a good thing. Overindulgence in alcohol, drugs, food, sex, and so on brings disease and poor health. Even extra or outside relationships bring unhappiness, problems and difficulties. A situation, often romantic, sours. In a reading where loved ones are involved, this card can indicate a marriage triangle, another man or woman the Seeker is involved with or concerned about in connection with the mate. Tread carefully before mentioning this. Check the section on "Card Combinations" to see if other infidelity cards are in the spread to reinforce this meaning. Someone may be talking behind the Seeker's back.

The Seeker is unaware of his or her natural abilities.

THREE OF SWORDS

One of the most dramatic cards in the Tarot deck is the Three of Swords. The heart of our feeling and emotional nature has been wounded. Sometimes we only grow through loss and misfortune. Although this card suggests that little can be done to save the situation, there is a silver lining to the bitter sadness, because growth will occur as a result of the necessary elimination. The card shows severing of a situation in the Seeker's life. Something must be forfeited because it has outgrown its usefulness. This can apply to persons, places or things. If this card appears surrounded by positive cards, suggest "cutting away of old to make room for new," sorrow of severance, or the necessary ending of a situation. Old attitudes, beliefs and situations must be cut away to make way for the new. This is a separation or divorce card. Also it shows severance as in surgery; this is good, for the necessary cutting will relieve the problem.

Reversed — The Three of Swords remains a severance card but the hurt may be less intense. Still, a separation occurs. The interpretation is similar to the upright. Often the individual is suffering less severely, either because the situation has occurred before (e.g., there have been repeated separations and reconciliations), or the severance or surgery is less intense.

THREE OF PENTACLES

The Three of Pentacles shows growth concerning jobs, talents, education and monetary matters. In this card we see the skilled craftsperson working with his talents in a professional capacity. His laboring on the inside of a church suggests interior or self-mastery, the conquering a situation in life. This card also indicates achieving competence in one's chosen field, promotion, recognition, prominence, degrees and certification.

Reversed — Half-hearted attempts and below average or average grades of workmanship are indicated. Generally, little effort or hard work applied to the situation. The Seeker displays only somewhat adequate, rather than exceptional, skills and ability.

Review of the Aces, Twos and Threes

COMPLETION

1. _____ is the basic meaning of all the Aces.
2. _____ can be found in all the Aces reversed.
3. Find the type of selfishness indicated in:
   a. Ace of Wands reversed _____.
   b. Ace of Cups reversed _____.
   c. Ace of Swords reversed _____.
   d. Ace of Pentacles reversed _____.
4. _____ is the key word of the Twos.
5. _____ is seen when the Twos are reversed.
6. Define the type of balance expressed in:
   a. Two of Wands _____.
   b. Two of Cups _____.
   c. Two of Swords _____.
   d. Two of Pentacles _____.
7. _____ is the basic theme of the Threes.
8. _____is seen in the Threes reversed.
9. How is lack of growth indicated in:
   a. Three of Wands reversed? _____.
   b. Three of Cups reversed? _____.
   c. Three of Swords reversed? _____.
   d. Three of Pentacles reversed? _____.
10. In the Ace, Two and Three of Pentacles we see the use of skills and abilities.
    a. What abilities would be required to bring about the Ace of Pentacles? _____
    b. Symbols of skill and cultivation in the Ace are _____.
    c. The qualities used in the Two of Pentacles are qualities of _____.
    d. This is symbolized by _____.
    e. The Three of Pentacles shows application of skills. What results have been achieved? _____
    f. This is symbolized by _____.
11. In the Ace, Two and Three of Wands we see growth of an enterprise or idea.
    a. The _____ of Wands is the actual idea.

   b. The _____ of Wands shows the putting
      out of the idea.

   c. The _____ of Wands shows results re-
      turning to the Seeker about the enterprise.

12. The Swords are the suit of mind and actions. Sometimes we
    can look at this suit and find mental action; at other times
    we see physical action, often both. Find both physical and
    mental interpretations.

   a. What kind of physical action do we find in the
      Ace? _____.

   b. What kind of mental action? _____.

   c. What physical action is seen in the Two of
      Swords? _____.

   d. Mental? _____.

   e. In the Three of Swords we find physical action
      concerning _____.

   f. The mental action suggested is _____.

13. In the Ace of Cups we find water symbolizing a flowing sit-
    uation.

   a. What is flowing in this Ace? _____

   b. In the Two of Cups these energies are flowing
      between _____.

   c. The Three of Cups indicates the growth and abundance
      of _____.

MATCHING
Upright Meanings

____ 1. A new, creative idea	a. Ace of Wands
____ 2. Necessary severance	b. Ace of Cups
____ 3. Putting out "feelers"	c. Ace of Swords
____ 4. The situation will materialize	d. Ace of Pentacles
____ 5. Communication between	e. Two of Wands
friends or lovers	f. Two of Cups
____ 6. Indecision, truce	g. Two of Swords
____ 7. Mastery	h. Two of Pentacles
____ 8. Understanding emotions	i. Three of Wands
____ 9. Growth in love	j. Three of Cups
____ 10. Results concerning an idea	k. Three of Swords
____ 11. Handling and balancing	l. Three of Pentacles
____ 12. Victory willed	

Reversed Meanings

____ 1. Little effort   a. Ace of Wands
____ 2. Nothing happens   b. Ace of Cups
____ 3. Forcing a situation   c. Ace of Swords
____ 4. Souring of a relationship   d. Ace of Pentacles
____ 5. Severance   e. Two of Wands
____ 6. No growth   f. Two of Cups
____ 7. Blocking feelings   g. Two of Swords
____ 8. Situation will not materialize   h. Two of Pentacles
____ 9. Venture encounters   i. Three of Wands
          difficulties   j. Three of Cups
____ 10. Decision, action taken   k. Three of Swords
____ 11. Arguments   l. Three of Pentacles
____ 12. Inability to handle situation

TRUE OR FALSE

____ 1. The Aces are the most important of the Ace through Ten, Minor Arcana card series.

____ 2. The hand symbolism of the Aces suggests creative forces.

____ 3. Lilies and roses symbolize good thoughts, desires and intentions that are pure and of a spiritual nature.

____ 4. The Ace of Swords' victory when this card is upright in a reading is achieved by brute force and pushing.

____ 5. The Ace of Wands requires discipline and willpower to carry the enterprise through to victory.

____ 6. The Two of Cups is a balanced relationship.

____ 7. The Two of Wands shows sincerity toward an enterprise.

____ 8. The Two of Pentacles advises one to resist changing conditions.

____ 9. The severance in the Three of Swords should be prevented.

____ 10. Talents and abilities are expressed and rewarded in both the Three of Cups and the Three of Pentacles.

Answers to the Review of Aces, Twos and Threes

COMPLETION

1. Beginning is the basic meaning of all the Aces.
2. Selfishness can be found in all the Aces reversed.
3. a. Wands — being demanding and unyielding.
   b. Cups — smothering of loved ones, inability to give love, giving conditional love, egotistical game playing.
   c. Swords — cruelty, forcefulness, threats, dictatorship, selfish aggressive action.
   d. Pentacles — selfish preoccupation with money, possessiveness.
4. Balance is the key word of the Twos.
5. Loss of balance (or imbalance) is seen when the Twos are reversed.
6. a. Wands — Balance between prior success and new venture; well-balanced desires and motivations.
   b. Cups — Balance between mind and emotions, passivity and activity, spirituality and practicality, male and female, passion and compassion, heart and mind.
   c. Swords — Balance between action and inaction.
   d. Pentacles — Balance within money situations (earning and losing, saving and spending, debits and credits), two business situations or jobs, or responsibilities in general.
7. Growth is the basic theme of the Threes.
8. No growth is seen in the Threes reversed.
9. a. Wands. An enterprise has not produced results.
   b. Cups — The situation sours.
   c. Swords — A loss is indicated. There has been failure or no growth.
   d. Pentacles — No growth in work, money, educational or practical matters because of lack of ambition or settling for "just getting by."
10. a. Ability in practical, hard work; planning; perseverance; financial carefulness; realism and responsibility.
    b. Symbols are the cultivated garden and the arbor, requiring skilled work and patience.
    c. Qualities of adaptability, flexibility, balancing and managing of more than one situation, business and/or financial matter.

   d. Qualities are symbolized by the character dancing and
      juggling, which require skill and agility and by the Infini-
      ty symbol that surrounds the two Pentacles.
   e. Skills have been mastered and now are being used suc-
      cessfully.
   f. The master craftsman working symbolizes applications of
      skills. He has been hired to perform his skills, and thus
      rewarded for his abilities.
11. a. Ace.
    b. Two.
    c. Three.
12. a. Physically willed and decisive action toward overcoming a
       problem; victorious action; determined action.
    b. It shows mind over matter, mental willpower.
    c. We see calling of inaction or the "time out."
    d. There is mental indecision.
    e. The card shows physical action concerning a severance.
    f. It suggests emotional weeding out or a mental house-
       cleaning.
13. a. Emotions, feelings and understanding are flowing.
    b. loved ones and friends.
    c. love and art (creativity).

MATCHING
Upright Meanings
1. **a**   2. **k**   3. **e**   4. **d**   5. **f**   6. **g**   7. **l**   8. **b**   9. **j**   10. **i**
11. **h** 12. **c**

Reversed Meanings
1. **l**   2. **e**   3. **c**   4. **j**   5. **k**   6. **i**   7. **b**   8. **d**   9. **a** 10. **g**
11. **f** 12. **h**

TRUE OR FALSE
1. t   2. t   3. t   4. f   5. f   6. t   7. t   8. f   9. f   10. t

Assignment Using the Aces, Twos and Threes

Lay out the following reading, using the Aces, Twos and Threes.

THE INDICATOR
Indicator Card — King of Cups

THE READING
Placement 1   Present Influence — Ace of Cups
Placement 2   Helps or Obstacles — Two of Swords
Placement 3   Past, Motivation — Three of Swords
Placement 4   Recent Past — Two of Cups
Placement 5   Possible Future — Ace of Swords
Placement 6   Immediate Future — Ace of Pentacles
Placement 7   Seeker's Attitude — Two of Pentacles
Placement 8   Others' Viewpoint — Two of Wands
Placement 9   Hopes and Fears — Ace of Wands, reversed
Placement 10   Final Outcome — Three of Cups

How would you interpret this reading? Use the interpretation section. Because you are beginning to learn interpretation of readings
with only Aces, Twos and Threes, the 12 cards are evenly distributed. There will not be a random fall of numbers or suits, so eliminate
card counting and suit assessment for now.

1 . The Indicator card is the King of Cups. What kind of man
   is asking the question? Describe him, referring to Court
   card information _____

   _____

2. What kind of questions could he have asked?_____

   _____

3. At Present the Seeker is experiencing _____

   _____

4.   _____
   may be helping or hindering his present situation.
5. He had _____ in his past.
6. Recently there has been _____.
7. He could possibly end up _____.
8. The next thing he will experience in relation to the question
   asked is_____.

 9. His attitude is _____
    on the matter.
10. Others see him as _____.
11. He fears_____.
12. The situation will conclude with _____
    _____

Answers for Assignment
Using the Aces, Twos and Threes

1. **He is honest, sensitive, sincere, kind and helpful**.
2. **A question about loved ones or an emotional matter**.
   He may be emotional or sensitive about his question. He approaches the inquiry with sincerity.
3. At present he is experiencing **a new understanding about himself and his feelings**. There is a positive breakthrough where he may be understanding others more fully as well as his own emotional nature. A love matter may be beginning.
4. **Indecision and choosing to remain inactive because of his emotions** may be helping and/or hindering him now. You and he could talk about this.
5. He had a **separation, sadness, or severance** in his past. His concerns about a loss in the past may be motivating him to ask the present question. He may be motivated to know if sorrow will happen again.
6. Recently there has been **a romance, a magnetic attraction between the Seeker and someone else**.
7. He could possibly end up **being decisive and taking action** in the form of willpower and determination toward the matter in the future. Victory may happen.
8. The next thing he will experience in relation to the question asked is **a new situation materializing or conditions stabilizing and coming together for him**. In this case the emotional matter may materialize or become a reality for him. The relationship may establish itself, bringing a new security.
9. His attitude is **adaptable, flexible and open to change** on the matter.
10. Others see him as **sincerely putting out efforts toward this matter**. Others see him as successful and looking for new goals to accomplish.
11. He fears **delays and setbacks in the venture**, and **selfishness either on his part or in another**. He fears that he is being too pushy.
12. The situation will conclude with **a happy ending**. The Three of Cups indicates a successful conclusion where love grows and the Seeker finds a mate. The Seeker may discover that the relationship will develop into permanency and there will be planning for a future together.

FOURS, FIVES AND SIXES
The Fours

Place the Fours, Fives and Sixes on the table. Looking at the Fours, you will find the basic theme of stability. In the Four of Wands, stability is easy to see. The people are celebrating the established completion of their labors. Because of the need for emotional stability, the character in the Four of Cups has retreated. Retreat is again the theme in the Four of Swords. The action we usually see in the Swords suit is stilled; the knight who represents us in life's battles is resting or suffering from "battle fatigue." His mind needs rest from worries and concerns. The Four of Pentacles' stability is apparent as we see the character sitting securely in a position of established prosperity.

FOUR OF WANDS

A floral garland, signifying fruition of goals, is secured with ribbons between four symmetrical wands. Two women hold high more fruits and flowers to show the joyous harvest they are celebrating. This is a harmony card, indicating projects completed happily and successfully. There is reward for efforts where peace and security are established around the Seeker's cherished enterprise. The victorious enterprise may be a relationship, home endeavor, profession or health.

Reversed — We find the same meaning applies. This is a restful card, one of blessings, appreciation and happy and successful completion. The enterprise has become victoriously established.

FOUR OF CUPS

In the Four of Cups, the Seeker retreats from emotional and mundane matters. He is tired and weary of exerting himself. The cups in front of him express this established security from successful previous efforts. The body language of the card suggests a closed position; a closed attitude to new opportunities or social involvements. This is a time of closing off, going into a shell, often withdrawing emotionally and retreating from showing one's feelings for a while. The Seeker has the luxury of time to sit back and look over life-style, job and financial state. The cup coming out of the cloud may indicate a new idea or circumstance the Seeker is contemplating or being offered. This new opportunity may be a very meaningful one, yet he does not reach out for it. Perhaps a new internal urge or dream has caused him to reexamine his values in life and to reassess his life's ambitions. This is a card of considering rather than taking action.

Reversed — The Seeker comes out of the shell and goes back into the world, ready to take on new adventures and opportunities. Here one opens up to people and feelings again and begins new liaisons. A relationship transcends itself for the better through honest assessment (e.g., from romance to friendship, or from parent-child to mutual respect of adult-adult). New aspirations emerge; new understandings take place with loved ones.

Sometimes this card can mean change within. It also represents the acceptance of social and family invitations.

FOUR OF SWORDS

The Four of Swords shows a knight resting from his difficulties and battles. His mind is also in need of rest, so he prays or meditates to raise his consciousness to a higher plane. When you see this card in a reading, the Seeker is in need of repose to recharge or regroup; advise him or her to take this necessary time out. This is a temporary truce; he will take up the sword lying by his side and confront his situation again in the future. The three swords on the wall suggest his previous victories. This is another retreat card that usually

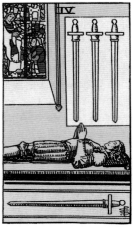

appears when one is in the middle of a difficult situation and knows all along that the problem is not over yet. A temporary truce has been called. This can be a recuperation card where the difficulties, health or otherwise, have ended and the Seeker needs some time for rest. He is in isolation, either self-imposed or created by circumstances and others.

Often this card, combined with other travel cards (Six of Swords, Eight of Wands and The Chariot) will indicate a journey for rest and relaxation. Meditation is mental rest and gives objectivity to the stressful situation. Therefore, if the Seeker cannot take a real vacation from difficulties, a mental one via meditation to gain perspective is advisable.

Reversed — This card, like the Four of Cups reversed, means renewed action. This time, because the suit is Swords, the action is aggressive and outgoing as well as mental in nature. Often this card reversed will indicate renewed action concerning a stressful situation. Though action begins, the Seeker should not go overboard. Perhaps he is ready to confront whatever conflict first caused the retreat. The Seeker renews an interest, romance, career, hobby or education matter from the past.

Strikes, walkouts, boycotts, layoffs, riots, looting and revolution can be indicated.

FOUR OF PENTACLES
The Four of Pentacles expresses the stability of an individual who has created personal economic security and enjoys its power. Disciplined organization brings financial security. Capricorn's motto of ''money equals power'' is represented in this card. Unfortunately, the individual here may find it difficult to share his wealth. Holding on to money is sometimes good, and the card means that the Seeker will have the money to hold on to (in moderation), and is therefore financially solvent. On the other hand, if there are other selfish cards around (Ace of Pentacles, Wands or Cups reversed; Six of Pentacles reversed; Ten of Wands reversed; Queen of Wands, Swords or Cups reversed; Knight of Swords reversed; King of Pentacles reversed)

then the Four of Pentacles depicts a situation where the individual is unable to give or even receive. From another aspect we see the individual may hold on too tightly in a situation.

Possessiveness is another meaning. It can be toward family members, other loved ones, or in business. This card indicates the inability to let go and delegate responsibility. At its best, it is a financial security card, having economic power and control in a situation. It is personal control and self-reliance to the point of closed, rigid, ungiving, distrustful, self-centered behavior: "My way."

Reversed — The opposite of maintaining power. We see the letting go or losing control of a situation although the Seeker very much wants to remain powerful.

We find loss of financial security through carelessness or letting money slip through one's fingers. In business and finance, problems and unavoidable interruptions victimize the Seeker. There is a feeling of powerlessness.

The Fives

The Fives are particularly dramatic in nature. Five is a number of change, and in each of the Fives we see disruption of the stability achieved in the Fours.

FIVE OF WANDS
Observe how the home security and harmony in the Four of Wands has been disrupted in the Five of this same suit. Here we see competition and strife, enmity and intense rivalry. Arguments and deliberate agitation cause changes. The Seeker will have to be courageous in fighting back.

Conflict in external conditions (e.g., friends, co-workers, family, and so on) is caused by divided opinions that bring disagreements over important issues. Occasionally some instigators may be insincere, creating problems for their own amusement.

In family readings, this card may show a strict authoritative male

causing hardship, yet it is the female's influence that motivates the male's actions. It also means internal fighting within oneself, feeling divided.

Reversed — Freedom from clashes and bickering. Peace and harmony reign. The situation will change for the better, but this requires the ending of the old ways and the beginning of the new. The routine ways of dealing with a situation are replaced by new and better methods of approach. Reorganization is successful. Sports, physical fitness and healthy competitive activities are also indicated.

FIVE OF CUPS

Remember the character in the Four of Cups? He was reevaluating and closed to new experiences. Perhaps he has decided to let go of an emotional situation, for the Five of Cups shows a loss. Often this card appears as a loss of a relationship, something breaking or ending very unhappily. When we apply the meaning of change, the number 5, to the suit of Cups, we can't help but find emotional matters unstable and leading to despair. Notice the mourning cloak and spilt cups that emphasize this loss. Also notice the cups left standing; they represent what the Seeker can salvage in his or her life although at this stage the Seeker may not be able to see this. When you are dealing with someone who has this card in a reading, advise the person to accept the loss. It really is a sacrifice for them and they may be bitter. Tell them to open their minds and focus on what they still have going for themselves. Sometimes this card can mean a loss, but a gain through taking the loss. Sacrifice can be the exchange of something lesser for something greater.

A romance, marriage or family may break up. The Seeker experiences emotional loss or disappointment or perhaps communication breakdown. Advise the Seeker to turn to the cups that are still full rather than dwelling on what has been spilt (lost). The Seeker should appreciate loved ones. Life still holds promise for her.

Reversed — This card improves in its reversed position, taking on the meaning of new hopes and the return of someone from the past. Usually the reappearance is positive. Not all is lost; the Seeker is filled with new confidence.

FIVE OF SWORDS

Storm clouds suggest difficulties. In the Five of Swords we see individuals defeated, victimized and taunted scornfully by a ruthless person. Revenge, cruel words and self-defeating actions tempt the Seeker to hurt someone else. Game-playing, scoring egotistical "points" and one-upmanship are the actions and thoughts of this card. Advise Seeker that they may get even or "score points," but revenge will be of little importance to them once accomplished. When you hurt another, you only hurt yourself. An alternative meaning for the card is getting something you thought you wanted and then no longer wanting it. The Seeker should question his motivations; they may be revengeful or self-defeating. This card indicates underhanded, unfair or even illegal methods the Seeker may consider using in order to get what he or she wants. Or the Seeker might fall victim to someone else's cunning and manipulation. There are plots and counterplots.

Reversed — This card's meaning remains the same: failure and loss, possibly at someone else's hands.

The Five of Swords is a tricky card because the victimization and loss could be caused by the Seeker or done to the Seeker. Sometimes the meaning will be apparent. At other times you may have to ask the Seeker which is happening.

FIVE OF PENTACLES

Poverty is the basic theme of the Five of Pentacles. Compared to the Four where we saw established stability, change here concerning

a secure matter could be a very unwelcome disruption and the harbinger of instability and misfortune. Here we find loss in every conceivable way; poor health is symbolized by the lame character; poverty is symbolized by the poor person; and spiritual disbelief is symbolized by the characters who ignore the church window above them. Loneliness and depression are also indicated. Perhaps this is a picture of what happens to the ungiving character in the Four of Pentacles!

Financially this is a poverty card — showing loss of money, job, income, and so forth. Emotionally, the loss of love brings loneliness. Loss of mental balance brings depression and negative attitude. The individual has lost something to care about and has abandoned his belief system. This person no longer has faith in whatever he once believed life was all "about."

In a medical reading, health difficulties are indicated.

Reversed — This card is much more cheerful reversed. We now see the poor souls with their faith or belief systems restored. The individual finds himself in part-time or temporary working conditions. He experiences better health. There is new involvement in religious or spiritual unfoldment.

The Sixes

Fortunately, balance is the theme of the Sixes in Tarot. Harmony is restored.

SIX OF WANDS

The competition seen in the Five of Wands has been overcome, leading to victory in the Six of Wands. Garlands, a parade and the central character riding high on horseback are all symbols that suggest the Seeker's triumph over the Five's strife-ridden conditions.

This is a card of accomplishment that celebrates the reward of victory achieved through effort and hard work. The Seeker triumphs in all endeavors, especially creative or ambitious ones. A leader has contended successfully and won out over the competition. Business dealings are victorious, or the individual is singled out as better,

superior or best-qualified. Here we see the Seeker reaping the results of persistence and popularity.

Reversed — This card reversed shows that achievement or advancement may go to another. A "second fiddle" card often appears in the reading of someone who feels unimportant compared to the loved one's work, family, or even extracurricular activities, (sport teams or hobbies). This can mean playing second fiddle to a third party in a marriage. Go carefully; before you mention this, look for other infidelity cards for reinforcement. Other infidelity cards are the Three of Cups reversed; The Empress reversed; two or more Queens; Kings or Knights coupled with these cards, or The Lovers reversed.

If the Six of Wands is victory upright, then reversed it means loss, failure, another person winning. At best, you can interpret it as delays in winning.

SIX OF CUPS

The Seeker's childhood, happy memories, reunions and cherished ideals from the past are represented by the children in the Six of Cups. Harmony is restored in family and emotional matters. Domestic love and felicity are symbolized here as in the Four of Wands. The Seeker's homeland (wherever he or she calls home), the purchase of items for enjoyment in the home and entertaining at home are all applicable interpretations. The past can hold wonderful memories as it does for the Seeker when the Six of Cups appears upright in a reading.

The celebration of special dates (e.g., anniversaries, birthdays, and so on) is indicated.

If it is next to a journey card (Six of Swords or Eight of Wands), this can be a "going home" card. It brings new chances to create emotional happiness or establish a harmonious home for oneself.

Reversed — Time for the Seeker to let go and stop dwelling on unhappy past events. The individual has to change and live for today. S/he has become old-fashioned to the point of rigidity, refusing to leave the past behind. S/he must weed out friends, situations or past loves, for s/he has outgrown them.

SIX OF SWORDS

The only way to regain balance in the Six of Swords after the failure and humiliation in the Five is to move away or leave the situation behind. We see the people, defeated and in sorrow, traveling to calmer waters (emotional balance). The troubled waters in the card's foreground represents their present loss.

This card can also indicate a change of attitude and seeing things in a new, more positive frame of mind. The Seeker is leaving problems behind, going away from previous hardships. Sometimes this is a physical change, i.e., moving, removal. The difficulty has ended or no longer touches the Seeker's life.

Reversed — No movement away from difficulties. Therefore, there is no journey or removal of problems. The Seeker will have difficulty changing his attitude concerning this situation, but that's all he can do. The Seeker is at a standstill.

SIX OF PENTACLES

Balance is suggested in the Six of Pentacles by the merchant's scales. This card can be interpreted as economic balance, a pleasant relief from the worry of the Five of Pentacles. The sharing of money, as well as fairness in financial matters, is indicated by the wealthy man giving to the poor. Investments prosper and return dividends. Sometimes this card can depict the giving of money as investment in someone, i.e., investing in a business, financing an education or saving for the recipient's future. The profit will be multiple. The Seeker is repaid and then some; the benefits and returns can manifest in money as well as personal satisfaction gained from helping people by contributing toward their future and watching them succeed.

In business or investing, the Seeker is advised to proceed

because profits will return. The scale symbolizes reaping and sowing and therefore the receiving of that which is deserved.

This card can also mean working in a career concerned with helping others.

Reversed — The Seeker does not get what s/he deserve. Instead, he or she experiences the unfair distribution of money, unethical or illegal financial situations, payoffs and coercion.

The Seeker may not receive what is rightfully deserved in wages, benefits, insurance claims, tax breaks, wills, stock dividends, contracts, agreements, buying and selling transactions, and so forth. Make sure the individual has the deal in writing and has read the fine print. Misrepresentation is possible.

Money and promises have "strings attached." There is financial manipulation.

Review of the Fours, Fives and Sixes

COMPLETION

The Fours

1. The basic meaning of the Fours is stability. We see retreat in order to establish emotional stability in the Four of _____.
2. Retreat is also seen in the Four of _____ where the individual requires time out before resuming battle.
3. Financial stability and secure power in a situation are represented by the Four of _____.
4. Harmony and the reaping of rewards lead to a stable home and success in the Four of _____.

The Fives

When we are in stable circumstances, we don't like the boat to be rocked by change and uncertainty.

1. In the Five of _____ we find our emotions upset because of an unwanted change concerning loved ones and affection.
2. The Five of _____ has had its stability destroyed by competition and agitation.
3. In the Five of _____, health, emotions, faith and wealth are suffering from undesired change.
4. The Seeker goes back into battle in:
   a. the Four of _____reversed and experiences defeat in:
   b. the Five of _____.

The Sixes

1. A balanced home and family are depicted in the Six of _____.
2. Balanced economic conditions are portrayed in the Six of _____.
3. Leaving a disaster behind is pictured in the Six of _____.
4. Victory brings new balance in the Six of _____.

ADDITIONAL COMPLETION

1. Competition
   a. The _____ of Wands is required to maintain the established stability seen in the
   b. _____ of Wands.
2. In the _____ of Wands this victory has been achieved.
3. What might happen if the Six of Wands indicated the future but fell reversed in the Seeker's reading? _____
   _____.
4. Optimism and new hope is seen in two of the five cards reversed. Which two? _____
   and _____.
5. Sometimes change can result in improved and harmonious conditions. Which Five reversed expresses this idea? _____.
6. Unfair and cruel tactics bring meaningless results in the Five of _____.
7. Two cards in the Fours represent going into a state of retreat; when reversed, they represent coming out of that state. Which two are they?
   _____. and _____.
8. The man in the Four of Pentacles holds on to his money. He has money on his mind (pentacle coming out of the top of his head), and bases his life on the security of his accumulated wealth (pentacles at the feet which are his base or represent his life's path). What happens to him when this card falls reversed? _____
   _____.
9. Name two ways the Six of Pentacles expresses the idea of sharing.
   a. _____
   b. _____
10. Symbols that represent sharing in the Six of Pentacles are
    _____.
11. Pleasant and happy memories are the interpretation of the _____ of _____.
12. Symbolized by _____
    _____.

MATCHING
Upright Meanings

____	1. Reunion	a. Four of Wands
____	2. Going into a shell	b. Four of Cups
____	3. Completion, reaping	c. Four of Swords
____	4. Victimizing	d. Four of Pentacles
____	5. Poverty	e. Five of Wands
____	6. Sharing and balance	f. Five of Cups
____	7. Power and money	g. Five of Swords
____	8. Retreat and meditation	h. Five of Pentacles
____	9. Success and conquering	i. Six of Wands
____	10. Leaving difficulties	j. Six of Cups
____	11. Loss in love	k. Six of Swords
____	12. Competition and fighting	l. Six of Pentacles

Reversed Meanings

____	1. New faith, part time job	a. Four of Wands
____	2. Failure, second fiddle	b. Four of Cups
____	3. Victimizing	c. Four of Swords
____	4. Return of loved one or friend	d. Four of Pentacles
		e. Five of Wands
____	5. Loss of control	f. Five of Cups
____	6. Unethical, unfair money	g. Five of Swords
____	7. Stuck	h. Five of Pentacles
____	8. Coming out of a shell	i. Six of Wands
____	9. Living in the past	j. Six of Cups
____	10. Action, an interest is renewed	k. Six of Swords
		l. Six of Pentacles
____	11. New harmony achieved through change, sports	
____	12. Reward, stability and peace	

Answers to Review of the Fours, Fives and Sixes

COMPLETION

The Fours	The Fives	The Sixes
1. Cups	1. Cups	1. Cups
2. Swords	2. Wands	2. Pentacles
3. Pentacles	3. Pentacles	3. Swords
4. Wands	4. a. Swords	4. Wands
	b. Swords	

ADDITIONAL COMPLETION

1. a. Five
   b. Four
2. Six
3. There would be a failure rather than success.
4. Cups and Pentacles
5. Wands
6. Swords
7. Four of Cups and Swords
8. He loses control of his financial security, becomes careless.
9. The idea of sharing is suggested by the interpretation of willingness to share with loved ones or invest in them. Also, sharing is indicated by working in a career of helping others.
10. Sharing is suggested both by scales that symbolize balanced giving and receiving and by the wealthy man sharing with the poor.
11. Six of Cups
12. The children (past, childhood) and their home behind them: flowers. The cup of flowers stands behind the child, a position suggesting that which went before — the past.

MATCHING

Upright Meanings

1. **j**   2. **b**   3. **a**   4. **g**   5. **h**   6. **l**   7. **d**   8. **c**   9. **i**   10. **k**
11. **f**   12. **e**

Reversed Meanings

1. **h**   2. **i**   3. **g**   4. **f**   5. **d**   6. **l**   7. **k**   8. **b**   9. **j**   10. **c**
11. **e**   12. **a**

Assignment Using the Fours, Fives and Sixes

Lay out the following reading, using the Fours, Fives and Sixes.

THE INDICATOR
Indicator Card — Page of Cups

THE READING
Placement 1   Present Influence — Six of Cups
Placement 2   Helps or Obstacles — Five of Swords
Placement 3   Past, Motivation — Six of Pentacles
Placement 4   Recent Past — Six of Wands reversed
Placement 5   Possible Future — Four of Pentacles reversed
Placement 6   Immediate Future — Four of Swords
Placement 7   Seeker's Attitude — Five of Pentacles
Placement 8   Others' Viewpoint — Four of Cups
Placement 9   Hopes and Fears — Six of Swords reversed
Placement 10   Final Outcome — Five of Wands

The Indicator is the Page of Cups, so you are reading for a young person. In this case it is a boy, a young man 16 years old. He has musical or artistic tendencies or appreciation. A natural talent could mature if he applies discipline. He is a kind, sympathetic individual.

Again we are omitting the customary general observations because only the Fours, Fives and Sixes are being used in this assignment.

1. His first card, indicating his present situation, is the Six of Cups. At present _____
_____.

2. His second card is the Five of Swords, indicating
_____ and _____ are
his obstacles.

3. In his past he experienced the Six of Pentacles, telling us his past experience has been _____.

4. But recently he has experienced the Six of Wands reversed, indicating that _____.

5. How he thinks his future may turn out is the Four of Pentacles reversed. Interpret: _____
_____.

6. The Four of Swords in his Immediate Future says he
   is going to:
   a _____
   b. _____
   c. _____
7. The Five of Pentacles is his attitude towards the matter,
   a. How does he view it?_____
   b. What is on his mind?_____
8. Other people see him as the Four of Cups. They will offer
   him _____ and _____.
9. The Six of Swords reversed shows that he fears _____
   _____.

10. The Final Outcome is indicated by the Five of
    Wands suggesting:
    a. _____ and _____ in
       his future.
    b. He could possibly lose control of his situation as
       suggested by the_____.
    c. Advise him to _____.

Answers for Assignment
Using the Fours, Fives and Sixes

1. At present he may have a question concerning the **harmony of his family life**. Right now he is asking about a home or family matter.
2. The Five of Swords indicates **victimizing** and **revenge**. Someone now influencing the matter may be fighting dirty and he may be tempted to do likewise. These are the conditions going against him.
3. The Six of Pentacles indicates his past experience has been one of willingness to share. He has had harmony through fair play. In the past **he has received what he felt was rightfully his**; this may be his motivation for asking the question. Will he receive his fair share this time?
4. Recently someone else involved in the family matter has won out over him or become the victor. He felt as if he were playing **second fiddle**. His needs aren't being met.
5. He thinks he may **continue to lose power and control** in the family situation.
6. a. **Retreat**.
   b. **Meditate, think or pray**.
   c. **Gain perspective**.
7. Mentally he **feels depressed, lonely and isolated**. He may be **questioning his faith or value system**.
8. **Understanding and support**.
9. He fears that **the situation will remain the same** and that no one's attitude will change.
10. a. **Contest and rivalry** between himself and another or others.
    b. Four of Pentacles reversed in the Possible Future.
    c. Expect contention and fighting. He may have to apply courage and defend himself. Some improvement may be derived from this Page **standing up for himself** and his needs.

SEVENS AND EIGHTS

The Sevens

The Sevens in the Tarot series provide interesting concepts. By now you should be able to get a feel for a card's meaning by its picture. One of the Sevens represents reevaluation and reassessment. One symbolizes dreaminess and indecisiveness, another, confrontation and yet another depicts betrayal and theft.

Seven represents the ending of a cycle and the unfolding of the soul. How are these ideas expressed in our Tarot Sevens? How did each cycle finish or conclude?

SEVEN OF WANDS

Confrontation is the major theme of the Seven of Wands. The character in the card is depicted on higher ground (having been the victor in the Six of Wands) and is confronting opposing circumstances from below. He has a superior vantage point and is maintaining his position with purpose and belief in himself.

In the Seven of Wands the Seeker feels very deeply about the position he is defending. His soul may be devoted to the continuation of the enterprise or venture, for he certainly has experienced ups and downs in attempting to fulfill it, as seen in the Ace through Six of this suit. The enterprise may have taken on great significance and meaning and now the soul which has grown through all the struggles, desires to continue and follow through. The purpose of this individual crusade keeps the Seeker competing, fighting and defending. His soul, the enterprise and its continuation have all meshed together, challenging the Seeker to experience his spiritual self. He now contends with courage and valor.

When this particular card appears in a reading, you can expect a situation to come to a head, to have to be faced. If the card falls in the Seeker's Past placement, the encounter has already occurred. The Seven of Wands in the Seeker's Present suggests that the confrontation is taking place now. If the Seeker is concerned about having to deal with a problem in the Future and this card appears, it would indicate that the situation will have to be dealt with head on. Disputes, competition and fighting in general are indicated.

Reversed — No confrontation is the Seven of Wands' reversed meaning. There still may be adverse, disturbing conditions around the Seeker but the anticipated confrontation will not occur. Sometimes this card can mean inability to "take the bull by the horns." The anticipated problems and disputes will not manifest.

SEVEN OF CUPS

In the Seven of Cups the Seeker's motivation and direction are not clear, even to himself. This is suggested by the dark shadowy figure in the foreground, indecisive about his desires. Each cup's symbolism refers to a different choice of lifestyle and motivation. He could go toward life's battles and win glory in fierce competition, suggested by the cup with wreath and skull. Temptation and jealousy, depicted by the snake and the dragon respectively, could be the foundation behind his choice. Wealth and securities, indicated by the home and jewels, may draw him. His dreams and ideals of the opposite sex are pursuits indicated by the head in the corner cup. On the other hand, the head could mean his coming to know himself. The final cup in the center suggests the unfolding, of his spiritual nature, the virtuous character he may discover himself to be. The point of this card is that none of the options is being chosen at this time. Therefore, we have the interpretation of confusion and indecision, perhaps because the Seeker has not yet come to know himself and his true needs.

The soul is the center cup in the Seven of Cups. We view it as the cloaked figure with the emanating aura. The harmony restored in the Six of Cups is assured and now the Seeker's soul cries out for unfoldment. Family life and the home are now settled, leaving room for the Seeker to grow in a new direction, his soul's direction, if he so chooses. Other dreams of attainment compete for his attention and he may ignore spiritual growth for more earthly goals.

The Seven of Cups can signify that the Seeker has illusions and fantasies about handling situations correctly or victoriously, when in reality, she is not. A lack of practicality and wasting time in dreaming rather than action are suggested.

Indulging in the worlds of unreality or escapism — television, books, alcohol, and so forth — lead to a serious excess, because of inability to cope with the outside world or realize the true self. If there are other cards of abuse with the Seven of Cups, then the individual may be involved with drugs or alcohol. Look for the Nine of Cups reversed and the Three of Cups reversed.

In a psychic reading, this card can be a significant dream or vision. A reading about psychic matters (e.g., a dream's meaning or the accuracy of a prediction), could include the Ace of Cups, and the Page of Cups (possibly with other members of the Cups court cards) as well as The High Priestess, The Moon and the Hanged Man.

Reversed — The Seven of Cups becomes the opposite of indecision. This time new goals and ventures are chosen and followed through. A good choice from all the possibilities is made and the individual has set his mind on following through.

SEVEN OF SWORDS

Self-betrayal and becoming one's own worst enemy are represented by the Seven of Swords. Often the Seeker may be unaware of this; s/he may act unconsciously to create circumstances of failure that bring about self-defeat. Perhaps the soul's lesson in this card is about being one's own worst enemy through thoughts and reactions. Negative, aggressive behavior and attitudes defeat the Seeker, who may be gaining the world but losing his soul. This cycle ends with trouble-making and mental game-playing winning out over the soul's needs.

The Seven of Swords brings renewed battling and problems after the journey away from troubles in the Six of Swords. In the Seven

it seems the old actions of victimizing and revengefulness have reemerged, resulting in the Seeker's taking advantage of a situation or person and refusing to face the outcome of the premeditated actions. This cheating and theft can take the form of stealing credit; undermining someone's work; cheating; or sabotaging a marriage, relationship, reputation, career or community standing. Actual theft can occur, or the damage may be created more subtly. The Seeker, as in the Five of Swords, can be the victim or the victimized. Again we see the character in the card stealing, but this time the theft occurs without the victims' knowledge. The people in the background of the Seven of Swords are occupied with other matters of battle (military camp). While they are busy, someone is taking advantage of their preoccupation, using that time to ruin, betray and slyly steal. In the Five of Swords the battle was open and the opponents came face to face; in the Seven, the damage may be done when the Seeker or victim is not looking.

Self-betrayal is one of the major meanings of this card. The Seeker may be taking action or making choices that will be self-destructive. Warn the Seeker not to trust the circumstances or people involved when this card appears. It shows something taken from one that no one has the right to take, or the Seeker could be the person contemplating or performing this unfair act.

Reversed — The Seven of Swords reversed is the apology card; credit is given where due and that which has been taken is brought back. The Seeker finds that appreciation due is given although this may be unexpected.

This is a card of capability. Constructive advice should be followed. The Seeker should become his own best friend by making positive, helpful choices.

SEVEN OF PENTACLES
A sense of failure and dissatisfaction is felt from the Seven of Pentacles. Something has grown through the Seeker's efforts, as represented by the pentacles growing on the vine. The Seeker has worked

hard and seen results but may not be satisfied. Perhaps his desires and motivations have changed and he no longer wants what he has been working on. This vine and its growth can represent years of the Seeker's efforts concerning marriage, career, finances, relationships, family, possessions or material matters. Something extremely important is missing: a sense of contentment or completion. He has achieved results but he may not want to pursue the goal further. The soul may be prodding him toward aiming higher with his career, material, educational and spiritual goals. But in this card the contemplation of these possibilities is as far as the situation has developed.

In a health reading, the Seven of Pentacles can indicate the internal malfunction of an organ or, problems with one of the body's systems through infections, imbalances, and so forth. This interpretation can be applied in both upright and reversed positions.

The Seeker recognizes a sense of dissatisfaction about his question. He compares his present position to where his goals should have taken him by now. He wanted to achieve more and may choose not to continue. Some results have materialized concerning a financial or career-related project.

Reversed — When reversed, the Seven of Pentacles indicates money worries, debts, mortgages, loan payments. Concern about them keeps the Seeker in a situation where he may no longer desire to be. This time, his efforts have brought little result; barrenness and loss may occur.

Health warnings still apply, as in the upright meaning.

There may be disillusionment with life.

The Eights

The number eight implies balance, success and power.

EIGHT OF WANDS

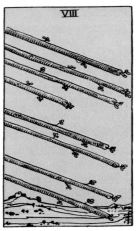

Remember the conflict and confrontation in the Seven of Wands? In the Eight the opposing wands have been removed, symbolizing the ending of opposition and freedom to move forward. The conflict has been resolved through the Seeker's valor and purpose in fighting for the venture's survival. Now the rewards are swift progress and fast results. The Eight of Wands is the green light, "all systems are go" card.

The Seeker is aiming toward an objective and its destination is near.

Ideas, dreams, expectations and aspirations are rapidly on their way to becoming reality.

A goal is being reached through devotion and dedication. Sometimes this devotion can be loving in nature. In an emotional reading this card expresses dedication toward loving and a loved one. Love can also be felt towards the venture the Seeker is pursuing, for the soul and its consecration are now involved.

Skill in sports, athletics, exercise, physical fitness and the Seeker's advocacy of such can be indicated also, with exercises beginning to take effect. Rapid progress, no interference and getting results are the basic interpretations of this Eight.

The Eight of Wands is a travel card, often travel by air.

Reversed — Obstacles, fighting and forcing an issue that shouldn't be forced are the Eight of Wand's reversed meanings. This card can mean violence in combination with other violent cards (Knight of Wands reversed, King and Queen of Wands reversed; Knight of Swords reversed; The Tower; Strength reversed; Ace of Swords reversed). Advise the Seeker not to push; the results could be destructive, producing quarrels and opposition.

When reversed, a trip may be interfered with.

EIGHT OF CUPS

Family and materialism have been the major considerations of the character in the Eight of Cups. The carefully stacked cups in the foreground depict his conscientiousness. There is a gap in the cups that represents something missing from the Seeker's life. Wearing the red color of desire, he turns his back on the cups that signify his present circumstances and begins a quest for something more personally fulfilling. Money, family and security are no longer satisfying; he searches for depth and meaning. Perhaps he has finally chosen to pursue the unfolding of his soul, taking the option presented in the Seven of Cups. The moon in this card symbolizes cycles. We see it full, indicating attainment and waning or decreasing, suggesting a decline of fulfillment in the material life. This life now abandoned, the Seeker begins to look for new significance and spiritual purpose. Emotional and family matters are left behind; relationships weaken and end.

The card is not so much the forfeiting or loss of power as it is a power exchange.

Having become disenchanted with the life of society and materialistic values, the Seeker chooses to embark on a new search for self-mastery.

The power, (number eight), he now pursues may be from a spiritual or ethereal source.

This card can also show unsatisfactory circumstances that cause the Seeker to give up a present involvement. It can show emotional disappointment in a loved one or with a love or family matter.

Reversed— Enjoying life's bounty of feasting, family, friends, relationships, social involvements and parties is the Eight of Cups' reversed meaning. A new relationship may be part of the abundance in the Seeker's life.

This is a party card; a social time with new acquaintances and flirtations. There may be a new love. Satisfactory circumstances bring enjoyment.

EIGHT OF SWORDS

A bound and blindfolded woman stands amidst a series of swords. If she could lift her blindfold to peer into the marshy waters beneath her, the reflection would be unclear.

The Eight of Swords has power (relating to the number eight) restricted. The Seeker does not recognize her own power to think or act. She allows others to interfere with her thinking and decision-making process while her own true needs are ignored. Her once- powerful actions are now fraught with indecision. Perhaps her excessive need for success and power and her aggressive actions toward achieving them have brought her to this present impasse.

Fear of taking a stand, speaking up for oneself or making a decision are manifestations of this card. The Seeker has been afraid of the choice for quite a while and can't see the way out; he or she is stuck until mental freedom is attained. Often this card appears when interference from others disrupts the Seeker's decision-making process. It indicates feelings of imprisonment, but the mental bondage is often self-inflicted.

Reversed — The caged bird flies free, the thinking process clears, interference decreases and action can be freely taken. Fear subsides, relief and release are felt in the matter.

EIGHT OF PENTACLES

The Seeker desires education in the Eight of Pentacles. Self-discovery, training for a job or studying a subject are some of the possibilities contained in this card. Basically the interpretation is "working on something," be it a relationship or a project. The character in the card is an apprentice learning on the job, involved in a work-study program or receiving some type of training. Potentials for better money and stability now exist. The Seeker may meet influential people or put his foot in the right door. The connections made and skills acquired can be capitalized upon in the future. Perhaps the forlorn man in the Seven of Pentacles has given up his former enterprise and has tried a new venture or at least attempted a different approach to his situation.

The individual in the Eight of Pentacles realizes that to achieve power in life, he must better himself. Being practical, he diligently sets out to improve himself to enhance his financial and economic future.

Motivated by money and material goods, he applies his efforts toward apprenticeship in a trade or profession. He is learning financial skill in handling money and becoming qualified and proficient at work.

Reversed — Circumstances within and outside prevent the pursuit of ambition.

The sincerity in craftsmanship witnessed in the upright Eight of Pentacles is nowhere to be found in the reversed interpretation. The individual here is quite good at what he or she does but may be frustrated.

The Seeker's ethics have become unglued; talents and skills remain but may now be put to devious use. Forgery, embezzlement, swindling, dishonesty, fraud, cheating and pretension still require skill and cunning.

Unfortunately the Seeker's overweening ambition may have caused him to become corrupt and manipulate his way to the top. Strings are pulled, hidden deals are made, kickbacks and under-the-table maneuvers are enacted.

Tax evasion, insurance swindling, forgery and cheating on exams are but a few of the many manifestations of the reversed Eight of Pentacles.

At other times, we simply find the less drastic meaning of wasting time at work or getting caught up in worrying, complaining or nit-picking concerning the question asked. Advise the Seeker not to be carried away with details at the expense of the overall, long-term view.

Review of the Sevens and Eights

MATCHING
Upright Meanings

_____ 1. Seven of Wands
_____ 2. Seven of Cups
_____ 3. Seven of Swords
_____ 4. Seven of Pentacles
_____ 5. Eight of Wands
_____ 6. Eight of Cups
_____ 7. Eight of Swords
_____ 8. Eight of Pentacles

a. Disappointment, abandonment
b. Reevaluation after much work
c. The "go-ahead" card
d. A situation must be faced
e. Betrayal from others or self
f. Studying or "working on it"
g. Success is unreal
h. Fearful thoughts impede actions

Reversed meanings

_____ 1. Seven of Wands
_____ 2. Seven of Cups
_____ 3. Seven of Swords
_____ 4. Seven of Pentacles
_____ 5. Eight of Wands
_____ 6. Eight of Cups
_____ 7. Eight of Swords
_____ 8. Eight of Pentacles

a. Following through on a new project
b. Freedom in thoughts and actions
c. The situation will not come to a head
d. Enjoyment of life's good times
e. Violence, misused force
f. Cleverness applied to underhanded activities
g. Money worries
h. Being one's own best friend

TRUE OR FALSE

_____ 1. The Seven of Swords can indicate self-betrayal as well as slyness and unfair treatment of others.
_____ 2. The Seven of Cups finds decision-making difficult.
_____ 3. Confrontations are unnecessary in the Seven of Wands.
_____ 4. Fulfillment and satisfaction with work is the Seven of Pentacles' major theme.
_____ 5. Pushing is necessary in the Eight of Wands reversed.
_____ 6. Clear thinking and positive actions are the Eight of Swords' basic interpretation.

_____   7. Nit-picking and getting caught up in details are the meanings for the Eight of Pentacles reversed.

_____   8. The character in the Eight of Cups may be pursuing a quest of his soul.

_____   9. The person in the Seven of Swords is aware of the revengeful plotting surrounding them.

_____ 10. The Seven of Cups is positive in a psychic reading indicating a psychic occurrence.

Answers to Review of the Sevens and Eights

MATCHING

Upright Meanings

1. **d**   2. **g**   3. **e**   4. **b**   5. **c**   6. **a**   7. **h**   8. **f**

Reversed Meanings

1. **c**   2. **a**   3. **h**   4. **g**   5. **e**   6. **d**   7. **b**   8. **f**

TRUE OR FALSE

1. True.
2. True.
3. False. They come to a head.
4. False. They are reassessing their work because of unsatisfactory results.
5. False. Forcing the situation could result in violence.
6. False. Clear thinking and positive action are this card's reversed meanings.
7. True.
8. True.
9. False. This plotting is hidden from him.
10. True.

Assignment

(See Lesson 8)

NINES AND TENS

The Nines

Nine is the number of <u>attainment</u>. It is the number about to reach completion in Ten, suggesting the idea of a cycle nearing an end. In the Nines we find some problems and difficulties are about to complete their job of bringing prosperity or destruction.

NINE OF WANDS

This Nine is known as <u>the defense card</u>. The individual in the Nine of Wands stands in a guarded position. His expression is wary and his head bandages reveal a prior battle.

He protects his rights through being prepared to defend and fight. He may have to contend again before his situation is secure. Often this card will appear when the Seeker may have to handle <u>another round of contention connected to a problem he has dealt with defensively before.</u> It can occur in many different situations, from a past relationship's return to upset the Seeker, to warnings of a reoccurrence of a past health problem. When this card appears in the Present or Future position, it tells the Seeker that, whatever the situation, the <u>problem isn't over yet and to remain watchful.</u> This warning will prepare the Seeker because this difficulty or similar circumstance has occurred before.

Here the individual is defending territory already fought for and won. The battle may concern individual rights at home or work, family and marital equality or personal character struggles. A reputation or important position must be shielded. The Seeker is still maintaining her rights. When this card appears, urge her to continue to be on guard, for a previous obstacle, fight or difficulty may recur.

In a health reading, this card can indicate resistance to health problems and a strengthened constitution.

Reversed — In reverse, the Nine of Wands becomes its obvious opposite: weakness and inability to stand up for rights that need defending. The Seeker is caught off-guard and hit below the belt, but really should have been more alert and prepared. The problem is from the past and has been encountered before. Through carelessness or plain cowardice the Seeker may have allowed past difficulties to dominate and overwhelm her.

The Seeker can correct this by keeping on guard for the surfacing of a previous problem. Sometimes the Seeker knows exactly what should be said, but inner fear prevents self-assertion. The obstacle or enemy could win out.

NINE OF CUPS

A happy, satiated man sits contentedly amidst his good fortune.

The Nine of Cups has attained sensual happiness. This is the "wine, women and song" card, suggesting good times, money, and enjoyment of the social, sensual aspects of life. Traditionally, the Nine of Cups is the wish card, promising the Seeker fulfillment of his desires.

The Seeker has good health and financial well-being. Life is enjoyed, but in moderation.

Reversed — The Seeker experiences disappointment about his wish. The attained happiness and pleasure could become lost. Perhaps overindulgence in the sensual, drug, or alcohol world has brought the Seeker to a state of financial loss or health abuse. Perhaps money, time and talents are being wasted through a life lived in seeking sensual pleasure and gratification. Gluttony and greed could characterize the Seeker.

NINE OF SWORDS

The Nine of Swords is about to reach ruin in the Ten of Swords. Perhaps the crying woman knows the end of her situation is coming and she grows sleepless with worry and despair. Those around her have experienced great losses and setbacks as well. Anything attained has been forfeited. The swords hang above her representing past conflict. Astrological trends are against her, symbolized by the quilt embroidered with astrology emblems. In alternate squares we see the red roses, symbols of her desires, attached to the squares of astrologically malefic or negative forces, indicating an undesirable outcome concerning her state of affairs. At the base of her bed a duel carved into the wood shows one soldier defeating another. Again we see life's battles in the suit of Swords. This time failure and the mental anguish of the victim are shown. The crying woman may have watched a loved one lose or may have been part of the battle herself. Perhaps she has been victimized, or she may have been the victimizer. In either case, mental cruelty and guilt could be the result. The Seeker is in such a state of despair that he or she must be told not to feel entirely at fault for whatever has happened!

The Seeker is suffering terrible mental torment — guilt, depression, anxieties and paranoia — often inflicted by an estranged loved one or cruel person in the Seeker's life. Threats and accusations have too great an influence; she may have lost self-respect. Confusion and self-hatred could be the results of this internal turmoil.

Reversed — The Nine of Swords reversed resolves the pain in the upright position nicely. Hopes, new faith and time help the Seeker to heal from the ordeal. I think of the Nine of Swords as the Scarlett O'Hara card. Upright we see all of Scarlett's pain, loss and suffering, possibly resulting from her own attitudes and the way she has acted (revengeful, cruel). Reversed, I'm reminded of the end of *Gone With the Wind* when Scarlett declares that ''Tomorrow is another day!''

Advise the individual to be patient and have faith; the problem will get better.

NINE OF PENTACLES

Attainment is suggested by the Nine of Pentacles in numerous ways. A garden has grown well, the grapes symbolize fruitfulness and the vine, trained on a trellis, suggests thoughtful cultivation. The character in the card has worked for these achievements and has been conscientious and careful in all endeavors. Financial gain, increase in security, stability, self-reliance and independence are the results. Self-confidence, the ability to know what is best for oneself and the wisdom to follow through with action are important qualities of this card. The bird signifies the mind and its wisdom; the individual controlling and training the bird has taught it to think wisely.

In employment readings this card represents an independent working situation, or a type of profession where one can control conditions.

Reversed — Deprivation enters the picture with the reversed meaning of the Nine of Pentacles. Generally this card indicates loss (upright, it indicates gain) in any situation the question covers. Foolish moves may be made, unwise action could be taken and the Seeker ignores inner advice and wisdom concerning the matter.

The Tens

The Tens of each suit reflect the idea of finished, ended or completed circumstances.

TEN OF WANDS

The man pictured in the Ten of Wands has ended up with heavy burdens of work and responsibility. Perhaps he should learn to delegate some of the load and refuse worries that are really not his to bear. He appears weighed down with backbreaking concerns. Still he perseveres, but some of his plans may not reach fruition. The card indicates oppression and sometimes failure concerning ambitions, often because the Seeker has bitten off more than he can chew. Enterprises and goals are not completed because of overcommitment on the Seeker's part that leaves no time to fulfill them. Warn the

Seeker of this, so that total failure can be avoided.

In a health reading we see back, spinal, muscular, skeletal and sometimes heart problems. Warn the Seeker about overextending himself or herself with worries, pressures, responsibilities and physical overexertion; these circumstances could bring illness.

A failure card: someone else's will could win out over the Seeker's.

Reversed — The Ten of Wands reversed still carries heavy problems and burdens but now the Seeker could be victimized by someone else's extreme ill will.

Another interpretation is that the Seeker could be pushing toward an egotistical goal and stepping on others.

The health interpretation of the card upright can still apply in the reversed position. Again a card of failure.

TEN OF CUPS

The completion depicted in the Ten of Cups is a happy one. The most significant symbol in this Ten is the rainbow, suggesting promises for tomorrow and protection of the Seeker's well-being in the present and future. This card is one of satisfaction. It is basically a family card, one of harmony and true love. Lasting situations — romantic or otherwise, blessed with stability and truth are the rewards indicated.

A great tranquility descends over the situation bringing contentment and fulfillment concerning the Seeker's question.

A marriage, partnership or union with the ingredients to keep it permanent and make it strong and stable may be indicated.

Reversed — The opposite of completion or satisfaction is seen in the Ten of Cups reversed. Now we find impermanent relationships, discontentment, lack of fulfillment and quarrel-filled circumstances. Often the relationship or project disintegrates. Family or marital disagreements can lead to disobedience and defiance.

TEN OF SWORDS

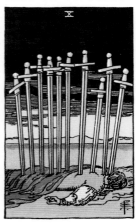

The picture is dismal in the Ten of Swords. We finally see the swords stab the character, symbolizing failure and disaster. The sky is black to represent bleakness; but not all hope is lost.

Ruin can be unexpected when it occurs in the last Sword card. This Ten is not always as disastrous as it looks. Plans that do not work out are represented here. These plans can be anything from a vacation to a career! At other times the failure can be quite complete, bringing loss and defeat to the Seeker. Perhaps the Seeker is receiving a culmination of previous thoughts and actions, reaping the results of a situation that was handled badly. At times the card will simply represent defeat that is not the result of the Seeker's wrongdoing.

A battle has been lost. The Seeker's plans and projects could fail. Hopes could come to naught and efforts fall short.

Reversed — The negative situation begins to get better. The Seeker may have changed his attitude or called upon higher forces for help. He or she is no longer relying on his own personal wit, cleverness and personality to get through rough times.

The power of prayer is used to overcome negative influences. A ray of hope brightens the Seeker's situation. Perhaps all is not lost. Problems begin to diminish.

TEN OF PENTACLES

The Ten of Pentacles is known as the wealth card. Stability, money and secure family conditions are completed in this Ten. The family suggests generations, ancestry and inheritance. Their wealth and position is obvious, symbolized by the estate and its abundance. Tradition, good lineage and reputation are important. When this card appears upright, all is in order and this standing is intact.

Large companies, corporations, big business and government may be places of employment, or the Seeker is dealing with such

a place or institution when the Ten of Pentacles appears.

In general the card is interpreted as firm, well established, strong conditions. Also, the card can suggest security and stability in any matter the Seeker asks about. Situations are being handled in the traditional manner.

The card also shows transition from one stage of life to another. This transition can be from single to married, dependent to independent, unemployed to employed; it can even be a change in income bracket or social status.

Reversed — We find the opposite of security. The reputation of the Seeker, his family or coworkers may be unfavorable or in jeopardy. Family or finances may be unstable. Dealings with big business or government may be fraught with difficulties and delays. All financial changes, especially concerning speculation, investing, selling, buying and dealing, should be avoided because of unstable economic factors (personal or national). All financial risks should be avoided.

Review of the Nines and Tens

COMPLETION

The Nines

1. Which one of the Nines represents failure?

   _____.

2. One of the Nines suggests defense concerning all that has been striven for. Which Nine shows the qualities of defense and preparedness? _____.

3. Emotional hopes and abundance have been attained in the Nine of _____.

4. We reach material wealth and prosperity coupled with great wisdom and self-reliance in the Nine of _____.

5. What do you notice about the symbolism in the Nine of Wands, and how does that reflect the meaning of the card?   _____

6. a. The Nine of Cups' body language suggests _____

   _____ .

   b. How does this relate to the meaning of this card?

   _____

   _____ .

7. The scene in the Nine of Swords clearly indicates

   _____ .

8. The woman in the Nine of Pentacles independently controls her thoughts and life as symbolized by _____

   _____ .

9. The Nines basically are negative cards in reversed position with the exception of

   a. The Nine of _____ reversed, whose meaning is

   b. _____ .

10. The Nines upright symbolize attainment; therefore, what we see in them reversed is lack of attainment or loss of fulfillment.

    a. What type of loss do we see in the Nine of Wands?

    _____

    b. How did it happen?   _____

    _____ .

11. a. Loss of _____ is incurred in the Nine of
        Cups reversed.
    b. How did it happen? _____.

12. What kind of loss has the Nine of Pentacles reversed expe-
    rienced?

    _____

    _____.

13. How could it have been prevented? _____

    _____.

The Tens

1. Two of the Tens suggest family security and stability. When
   falling reversed they indicate family problems and instability. These two Tens are _____
   and _____.

2. In our other two Tens failure is incurred. They are the Ten
   of _____ and _____.

3. In one Ten in particular we find health problems: the Ten
   of _____.

4. a. What kind of health problems could occur?

      _____ .

    b. How could they happen? _____

      _____ .

5. a. In the Ten of Wands reversed the situation has

      _____

      _____ .

    b. What new force has been introduced and what has
       happened _____

      _____ .

6. The other negative Ten, the Ten of Swords, improves when
   reversed. What kind of improvement has happened and
   how? _____

   _____.

7. Both the rainbow in the Ten of Cups and the archway in the
   Ten of Pentacles have the same curving, overhead shape.
   a. What do the two symbols represent?_____

      _____ .

    b. How does this apply to the two cards' meanings?

      _____

      _____ .

MATCHING
Upright Meanings

_____ 1. Nine of Wands   a. Wisdom brings independence
_____ 2. Nine of Cups   b. Guilt, mental cruelty
_____ 3. Nine of Swords   c. Burdens become overbearing
_____ 4. Nine of Pentacles   d. Failure concerning projects
_____ 5. Ten of Wands   e. Tradition and transition
_____ 6. Ten of Cups   f. Guarding and alertness
_____ 7. Ten of Swords   g. Satisfaction
_____ 8. Ten of Pentacles   h. Wishes come true

Reversed Meanings

_____ 1. Nine of Wands   a. Healing
_____ 2. Nine of Cups   b. Instability
_____ 3. Nine of Swords   c. Ruinous, premeditated actions
_____ 4. Nine of Pentacles   d. Disobedience, quarrels
_____ 5. Ten of Wands   e. Loss, ignoring inner advice
_____ 6. Ten of Cups   f. Overdoing and excess
_____ 7. Ten of Swords   g. Caught off guard
_____ 8. Ten of Pentacles   h. Prayer brings relief

TRUE OR FALSE

_____ 1. Government work or employment in larger, well-established companies is an interpretation of the Nine of Pentacles.

_____ 2. Independent employment, where one can determine hours and schedules, is attributed to the Ten of Pentacles.

_____ 3. Life's good times, filled with wonderful food, company and social riches, are the Ten of Cups' basic meanings.

_____ 4. Meaningful relationships and permanent, satisfactory circumstances are associated with the Nine of Cups.

_____ 5. The Nine of Wands reversed warns us to be armed and prepared to handle a previous difficulty come again.

_____ 6. Finances reach a standstill or possibly even reversal in the Nine of Pentacles.

_____ 7. The power of prayer and the overcoming of ruin are the interpretation of the Nine of Swords.

_____ 8. Loss, mental confusion and paranoia, over which the Seeker has little control, are qualities of the Ten of Swords.

Answers to Review of the Nines and Tens

COMPLETION

The Nines

1. Nine of Swords
2. Nine of Wands
3. Nine of Cups
4. Nine of Pentacles
5. The bandaged man suggests prior conflict. The character appears **on guard and has taken a stance of defensiveness**, which is the meaning of this card.
6. a. The body language is the folding of arms as if to say "Look what I've got!" He obviously is **pleased and gratified**.
   b. This concept relates directly to the card's meaning of **abundance in material and social matters**.
7. The scene in the Nine of Swords clearly conveys **suffering and crying in despair**, the card's major meaning.
8. **The bird**, a symbol of her mind, **has been tamed**, suggesting skill in controlling attitude, thoughts and thinking habits.
9. a. Swords
   b. **New hope and healing through time.**
10. a. The loss is one of **rights and position**.
    b. Setbacks have occurred because the Seeker was **caught off guard** or simply couldn't speak up for himself (cowardice).
11. a. **Loss of money and love, also pleasure**, has occurred in the Nine of Cups reversed.
    b. It happened through **wastefulness, overindulgence and gluttony**.
12. The Nine of Pentacles has experienced financial loss and **loss in general**. The loss is also in **confidence and faith in personal wisdom**.
13. This may have been prevented by being more cautious and **listening to the inner self**.

The Tens

1. a. Cups
   b. Pentacles
2. a. Swords
   b. Wands
3. Wands
4. a. **Spine, heart, back, skeletal and limb problems**.
   b. They are caused by **handling too heavy a burden**, either mentally or physically, sometimes both. They can be prevented through carefulness, no pushing or overexertion.
5. a. **Become worse**.
   b. The new force is **someone else's selfishness**, manipulation and demands, resulting in the defeat of the Seeker's situation.
6. Negative conditions are lessening in strength; this may have happened through **prayer or change of attitude**.
7. a. The symbols **signify protection and assure continuation of present security and harmony**.
   b. The two cards both have interpretations of **lasting and protected family** (Ten of Cups) and **stable family plus secure monies** (Ten of Pentacles).

MATCHING
Upright Meanings
1. **f**   2. **h**   3. **b**   4. **a**   5. **c**   6. **g**   7. **d**   8. **e**

Reversed Meanings
1. **g**   2. **f**   3. **a**   4. **e**   5. **c**   6. **d**   7. **h**   8. **b**

TRUE OR FALSE
1. False. It is the Ten of Pentacles.
2. False. It is the Nine of Pentacles.
3. False. It is the Nine of Cup's basic meaning.
4. False. It is the Ten of Cups.
5. False. In the Reversed position we are unprepared.
6. False. This is the card's reversed meaning.
7. False. It is the interpretation of the Ten of Swords reversed.
8. False. It is the Nine of Swords.

Assignment

(See Lesson 8)

ASSIGNMENT FOR SEVENS, EIGHTS, NINES AND TENS

We again omit number assessment and suit count because we are using only the Sevens, Eights, Nines and Tens. However, we have included the **Cut** so that you may begin to familiarize yourself with this part of the reading.

THE INDICATOR
1. The Indicator is the Queen of Pentacles. Interpret:
   _____
   _____.

THE CUT
1. In the Past fell the Nine of Wands reversed, indicating
   _____
   _____.

2. The Present is the Seven of Cups. Interpret:_____
   _____.

3. The Future is the Eight of Swords reversed. Interpret:
   _____
   _____.

THE READING

1. Placement One — At Present the Ten of Swords is being experienced. Interpret: _____
_____.

2. Placement Two — Obstacles are seen in the Seven of Wands crossing the Seeker. Interpret: _____
_____.

3. Placement Three — The Past holds the Eight of Cups reversed.
   a. Indicating _____
   b. How does this motivate the Seeker's question? _____
   _____ .

4. Placement Four — Eight of Wands reversed. What has happened recently? _____
_____.

5. Placement Five — Possibly the forces suggested by the Ten of Wands reversed could affect the future.
   Explain: _____
_____.

6. Placement Six — The Seven of Pentacles will be happening next, suggesting: _____
_____.

7. Placement Seven — Nine of Pentacles reversed tells us this is on the Seeker's mind: _____
_____.

8. Placement Eight — Ten of Cups. The Seeker's friends and family are:

   _____
   _____.

9. Placement Nine — Hopes are expressed in the Nine of Swords reversed. This indicates: _____
_____.

10. Placement Ten — Seven of Swords reversed. The end result of the question will be: _____
_____.

Answers for Assignment
Using Sevens, Eights, Nines and Tens

THE INDICATOR
1. The Queen of Pentacles **is a secure woman** or a woman asking a question about her security. Her inquiry may possibly concern a financial or job-related matter because she chose the Pentacles.

THE CUT
1. The Nine of Wands reversed indicates that in the past she experienced some adversity that she did not foresee. Perhaps she thought a problem was behind her, but it came back and hit her when she was least expecting it. She was **overwhelmed and unable to defend herself**, allowing herself to be dominated by the situation.
2. The Seven of Cups in the Present shows that **uncertainty plagues her**. Her emotions cloud her thinking and her **reasoning is unsound, unclear**. She may be unsure of what she wants; her needs seem hazy and undefined. A warning may be connected with thinking that she now has a grip on her problem when in reality she may not. She cannot choose what to go after in life and is uncertain about her priorities and motivations, so she chooses nothing.
3. The Eight of Swords reversed in the Future tells us that she will **free herself from the present indecision and liberate herself from fears**. There will be movement.

THE READING
1. At present she is experiencing the Ten of Swords, suggesting that she is asking about **a condition of ruin or failure**.
2. The Seven of Wands describes **obstacles and the confrontation of them**. The Seeker is presently dealing with adverse conditions. Opposing circumstances have come to a head and the Seeker finds herself challenged by them. She has courage and valor to confront them and defend her position, and that will help her. Difficulties requiring a showdown are the Obstacles or Hindrances in the matter.
3. Her Past is the Eight of Cups reversed, showing that she has
   a. **Experienced good times and easy conditions**; and
   b. may be motivated to ask if carefree times will ever return.

4. The Eight of Wands reversed describes a recent situation filled with pressures. **An issue may have been pushed at the wrong time**.

5. Possibly she could encounter more domination and opposition in her future. **Someone could victimize her further**; her future could still be negatively influenced by interfering, manipulative forces.

6. She will be doing some serious soul-searching and reevaluation in the immediate future. Sensing something missing in her life, she will take the time to pause and reflect on her work and question whether she should continue. **Perhaps her goals have changed**.

7. Mentally her outlook is insecure. She feels **unable to trust or tap her own wisdom on the matter**. She is thinking about losses.

8. Her **friends and family are comforting**. They may stand by her and be her protection and safety in this very unsettled period of her life. Another way of looking at this placement could be that friends and family see her as safe and in satisfactory conditions. I would tend to choose the first interpretation, because the general tone of her reading is one of disaster and conflict. Chances are her family and friends would know her dilemma and offer her refuge.

9. **Time helping to heal her situation** and her feelings of new faith returning.

10. That in the future the Seeker will be competent in handling new situations and will be receiving an apology. **She will become her own best friend, making sure she chooses a constructive, helpful path for her future**. She may receive positive and helpful advice and follow it. In comparing this Final Outcome to the Possible Future, we see cards of opposite type. In this case, take the meaning of the Possible Future card as advice in avoiding pitfalls. With the Ten of Wands reversed, we would warn her to watch out for future manipulation and unfairness from others and to guard her plans. The future looks brighter when we remember the Future card from the cut, the Eight of Swords reversed. This will bring her liberating circumstances; possibly she will free her mind and take action to help herself and seek counseling. (Seven of Swords reversed). Mentally she will become free of fears and interference from others, There may be the overcoming of the domination that has been a theme throughout her reading (Nine of Wands reversed, Eight of Wands reversed and Ten of Wands reversed).

THE COURT CARDS

Rules for Interpreting the Court Cards

When Court cards appear in a reading: **Ask the Seeker if the question involves other people.**

He or she may have asked a question about what another person or persons might do in the future. Another strong possibility when Court cards turn up is that the Seeker is inquiring about a situation between himself and another person.

The Seeker may confirm that others are involved or may tell you, "No, there are no other people involved with the reading and basically it concerns only myself."

This is your first step in interpreting the presence of Court cards. From this point when the Seeker has answered affirmatively or negatively to your inquiry, whether others are involved in the question, you can proceed to interpret the Court cards correctly.

When Others Are Involved

If the Seeker has revealed that there **are** others involved in the query, **interpret the Court card using (a) the placement in which it has fallen and (b) the particular character attributed to that card.**

a. The placement (e.g., Present Influence, Hopes and Fears, Final Outcome, and so forth) reveals **when** this individual is or was involved with or influenced the Seeker's question.
b. The character description defines **who** the person is in the Seeker's situation.

An alternative to asking beforehand if others are involved, is simply to deal with the Court card when you arrive at it during the reading. Refer again to the character and placement for your interpretation. When you read the Court card, again referring to personality and placement, ask if the Seeker recognizes this character as another individual linked with the question or as a description of the Seeker himself.

EXAMPLE ONE
The Queen of Pentacles reversed has fallen in the Seeker's Recent Past placement.

Reader: "Are there other people involved in your question?" or "There seem to be other people involved in your question. Is this correct?"
Seeker: "Yes, there are others involved."
Reader: "The Queen of Pentacles has fallen in your Recent Past placement. This indicates an unstable, insecure woman filled with fears and self-doubt who has recently influenced or affected your question. Is this you or a woman around you?"

At this point, a cooperative Seeker will advise you whether your interpretation suggests their own recent behavior or that of another.
If the Seeker is uncooperative, unwilling to fill you in on the question, handle the situation by simply stating, "There was an unstable, insecure woman influencing the question recently. This may be you yourself or another woman recently involved with your question." Continue with the reading.

EXAMPLE TWO
The King of Cups is in the second position of Helps and Obstacles. We always read the card falling in the second position as upright. The first card, placement one, of Present Influences is also considered because we read placements one and two in conjunction with each other. The Present Influence card is the Two of Cups. The Two of Cups immediately suggests a question of an emotional nature. Presently the topic is of romance and the sharing between friends and loved ones.

Reader: "You have the Two of Cups in the Present Influence placement. At present you are asking a question about a relationship or the sharing between yourself and another. The King of Cups is the second card of Helps and Obstacles. Have you inquired about a man who is mature, emotionally stable, kind, understanding and easy to talk to? Does he have influence in the question?"

Seeker: "Yes. There is a man fitting that description."

Reader: "Because the Suit of Cups appears in both placements of Helps and Obstacles and the Present, I feel you have strong feelings for him and find him a helping force in your life."

If the reading has upsetting cards in it, especially the Present Influence card, the King of Cups crossing the Seeker could indicate a man whose character the Seeker may be questioning; or the Seeker is finding that this man is creating obstacles or oppositions. Look to the Future cards to reveal whether he will be trustworthy or unreliable.

When the Reading Concerns Only the Seeker

When the Seeker's question is about himself or herself, read the Court card as the Seeker's character. Again, refer to personality as described by the Court Card and its placement. Use the *Character* description as the Seeker's identity. Refer to the placement to indicate *when* they express this personality.

The question may not deal directly with others. The situation inquired about may deal with the Seeker's self-identity or self-knowledge. Perhaps the Seeker wishes to know how to handle the question, what qualities to use for deeper self-understanding or how best to handle circumstances.

These are other examples of a question involving only the Seeker; "What will happen in my career?" "How will my investments turn out?" "What will happen if I move?"

EXAMPLE

The Knight of Pentacles reversed in the Past placement could be interpreted as a man — the Seeker, in this case — who was careless and financially unethical in the past.

The Knight of Swords in the Immediate Future could still indicate the Seeker, but with an internal change of character or attitude. The Knight of Swords tells us that the Seeker will be strong-minded, aggressive and quickly decisive in the Immediate Future.

The Page of Pentacles in the Seeker's Attitude placement shows that he is open-minded and willing to learn.

All of these Court characters can appear within one reading and still indicate the personality of the Seeker in handling the question rather than other people.

If the Seeker answers ''No'' to your query of others' involvement, Court cards in the Future positions could indicate the Seeker's future personality or character traits in handling the question. A Court card in a Future placement may indicate that the Seeker's future does hold another person who will contribute to future circumstances that the Seeker may have no present knowledge of.

Additional Rules for Interpreting Court Cards

Pages are also personality traits of the Seeker.
When **Knights** appear they may indicate **events** of **importance**.
Pages in a reading can be **events** and **circumstances**.

Pages are **messengers**, and in our Tarot deck the **communications we receive** — verbal or written, formal and informal — are heralded by their appearance.

In **parenting** and **family** readings, **Pages** personify the **children**. Character qualities as well as lifestyles and career potentials of the child are interpreted from the description of the Page.

When a Court Card Appears in Placement Ten

Whenever a Court card upright or reversed appears as the Final Outcome card in placement ten, turn over the following or the eleventh card. A Court card in the tenth position indicates that a person or an aspect of the Seeker's character described by that Court card will determine the outcome of the circumstances.

EXAMPLE ONE
The Knight of Swords reversed for the Final Outcome would indicate a man making a quick, unexpected exit from the situation. This man's unfair threatening or leaving could be how the Seeker's situation finally concludes. A Court card in the tenth position, therefore, tells us a **person will bring the question to its conclusion**. The next card in sequence, card eleven, is the Six of Wands reversed, which explains **what that person is going to do**. In this case the Knight of Swords reversed will cause him or her to feel second-rate,

or bring failure to the Seeker by choosing someone or something over the Seeker. If card eleven is another Court card, move on to the twelfth card or until you find the event, indicated either by a Major Arcana or one of the Ace through Ten cards of the four suits.

EXAMPLE TWO

Another example is a business reading. The Page of Wands has emerged as the Final Outcome in placement ten, indicating enthusiastic messages and also energetic, courageous character traits expressed in the future. How this message will turn out, what the application of these personality traits will bring is revealed in the eleventh card, the Six of Pentacles. It indicates that the Seeker will reap rewards and benefits financially and achieve balanced and beneficial conditions by sharing.

THE COURT CARDS — PAGES AND KNIGHTS

The Pages

In studying the "Rules for the Court Cards," we found that the Pages can represent people and their characters. With the Pages there are definite personality traits that can be applied to the Seeker or to the character of someone involved in the Seeker's question. If the reading is about a child, then we take the Pages as representing that child and his or her disposition. Also, in readings for a family question, the Pages indicate a child and its character, either boy or girl.

In readings involving other people — coworkers, relationships, and so on — the Pages refer to the character of the person involved, or qualities the person may be expressing in the context of the question asked. For example, the Page of Wands in a reading about a social club could indicate a full- steam-ahead, daring attitude of club members or of the Seeker.

The Page of Swords appearing in a reading about work and coworkers would indicate applying the qualities of diplomacy, adaptability and communication to the situation.

The Pages can also represent events. Read the Pages in the context of the question asked. The Page of Wands is a dynamic, spontaneous event. The Page of Cups is the conception of a creative idea. The Page of Swords is an occurrence connected with spying in general, and the Page of Pentacles is a learning or educational event.

Another possibility represented by a Page's appearance in a reading is a message. The suit indicates the character or the type of message. The Page of Wands indicates favorable news or messages. The Page of Cups is an inspirational message. The Page of Swords is an upsetting message. The Page of Pentacles is an informative message.

PAGE OF WANDS

PAGE of WANDS.

The Page of Wands has the qualities distinctive in all the Wands people: enthusiasm, energy, personality, outgoingness, giving, competitive, ambitious and courageous. This Page takes chances and is quite attractive and intelligent. Such people love appearing in the limelight and expressing their natural leadership ability.

The fire colors, indicative of the fire signs of Aries, Leo and Sagittarius, are represented by the Page's red, orange, yellow and gold attire. Because the youth belongs to the suit of fire, he or she is ambitious and capable of great courage, energy, and leadership.

Either children or adults can additionally be described as competitive, ambitious, impulsive, magnanimous, innovative and needing to be the center of attention. Performing, coaching, athletics, promoting, politics, sales, teaching and dealing with people are all different avenues this Page can embark on to seek out the limelight.

When dealing with messages from this Page, we find an encouraging message itself can be indicated in the upright position — a phone call, letter, word of mouth, and so forth.

If an event, it means springing forth with daring and determination in a new venture.

Reversed — The Page of Wands reversed will do just about anything to get attention. Sometimes we find misbehavior or destructive action out of the need to feel cared for or loved. The unbalanced need to be noticed or important drives the individual to stoop to unethical or theatrical means. The character becomes a braggart, makes mountains out of molehills, exaggerates and can be jealous. The individual overdramatizes and becomes temperamental, regardless of age.

If the Page of Wands reversed is next to a Knight or King reversed, and the reading is of romance, a man may influence the relationship unhappily.

Brokenheartedness can be an event associated with this card if the reading is emotional.

In messages, we can encounter unfavorable news and upsetting information.

PAGE OF CUPS

PAGE of CUPS.

The Page of Cups depicts the astrological water element of Cancer, Scorpio and Pisces with his flowing, magnetic, soothing and responsive nature. The connection is easily made to the emotional and feeling concepts associated with the Cups Court people; love and emotions flow, comfort, attract and respond.

Water is also strongly suggested in the Page of Cups as we see the youth garbed in the colors of the sea; blues and greens. Water rolls behind her or him and we discover a sea creature, a fish, emerging from a chalice.

Qualities of character in both children and adults, applied to the Page of Cups and all the Cups Court people are sympathy, sensitivity, imagination, lovingness, kindness, artistic ability, and intuition. Artistic , creative or humanitarian talents could be developed into a profession through training and self-discipline. Encourage discipline, classes and seeing this talent through to fruition.

The Page of Cups can represent an idea, creative thought or dream that the Seeker is contemplating, symbolized by the fish rising from the cup.

An inspirational or psychic message can be indicated by this Page, as well as a birth or marriage announcement, or an important communication that stimulates creativity.

Reversed — This Page requires discipline concerning his or her talents. Such persons may be living in a world of their own, running away from reality through alcohol, dreaming, drugs and escapist activities in general. The Page may drop out of society and become reclusive rather than cope with making friends and having a social life. Fearing rejection, these people grow insecure and retreat.

They may indulge in dreaming or wasting time, becoming

irresponsible. Their talents are not being used. This Page can indicate a lovable but easily spoiled person who expects too much and gives too little.

The Page of Cups may be receiving intuitive or inspirational messages but not heeding them.

PAGE OF SWORDS

PAGE of SWORDS.

Notice how the air signs of Gemini, Libra and Aquarius, and their intellectual and animated qualities are accentuated in the suit of Swords by the Court cards. Action is equally important to these people, and often they will enjoy games and interests that combine mental alertness and agility with physical assertion and dexterity. For example, martial arts, skating, swimming, and gymnastics are skills that combine mind and body. The wind blows through this Page's scene and the sky contains birds (ideas) and clouds, suggesting exciting, unpredictable, changing circumstances. The breeze wanders hither and thither as do the Page's interests, mental attitudes and opinions.

Qualities of diplomacy, adaptability, agility and flexibility are signified by the Page of Swords. Communication fields, science, technical or engineering careers can be indicated, as well as aptitude in languages: foreign, computer, mathematical, technological or scientific. Aviation, space, acrobatics, gymnastics and travel jobs are associated with the Page of Swords.

This individual may have two occupations, even simultaneously. They need activity, challenges and changes within their daily routine and enjoy mental games and pursuits.

This character requires much cerebral excitement and is always looking for new, stimulating topics to learn about. These people become bored easily and tend to leave projects unfinished.

Strong, with a curious intellect, this child talks and walks early or quickly.

If the card indicates a message, it contains unexpected news.

The event of spying is related to the Page of Swords.

Reversed — In Page of Swords reversed, the intellect becomes too sharp, causing the person to be cruel and critical with a manipulative, sarcastic, cynical, suspicious and accusatory nature. Purely intellectual, this reversed Page believes nothing and questions everything.

It shows circumstances where the true identity of a person or situation will be exposed. Or, the Seeker will see a person or situation as it really is.

Character qualities in this reversed Page can be fickleness, craftiness, sarcasm and unpredictability.

Both upright and reversed positions carry the interpretation of unexpected news of an upsetting nature. Advise the Seeker to be prepared.

PAGE OF PENTACLES

The earth signs of Taurus, Virgo and Capricorn are personified by the Page of Pentacles. These people are close to the Earth, nature-loving and down-to-earth, believing in duty and the practical, materialistic world. Quiet and reflective, this Page is contemplative; perhaps "still waters run deep."

Possessions are worked for and cherished; goals are realistic and hard-won. Earth colors of brown and greens are worn by the Page and flowers bloom in a field, suggesting the bounty and continual creativity of earth sign people.

Patience, openmindedness and regard for others' view-points are indicated here. Carefulness and caution are other character traits, along with timidity, respect for authority, conformity, responsibility, persistence, and broadmindedness toward all people.

The Page of Pentacles expresses the ability of studying or learning. It represents a student of any age or the ability to learn from situations. This can mean formal study or a person who looks at life as a learning experience. The Page of Pentacles believes a lesson is to be learned in all things.

It shows messages of an informative nature that we learn from.

Events are connected with learning; the person approaches the situation with an open mind.

Reversed — We find rebelliousness, isolation (possibly self-imposed), misunderstanding, carelessness, extravagance and self-pity. Another negative character trait is the inability to learn from others or even from personal experiences and mistakes.

Other traits can be qualities of revolution, nonconformity, refusal to compromise, and feeling the world is against one.

This position also shows learning problems or rebellion against parents, authorities and education.

Informative messages may be disregarded or ignored.

The Knights

Knights are very important in Tarot. Of all the Court cards they carry the most influence, just as the Aces are the most significant in the Minor Arcana.

The Knights are not as confusing as the Pages because usually they represent people — young men between 18 and 35 years of age, roughly speaking. There are exceptions: an adolescent who is mature for his age will appear as a Knight; an older man, youthful and energetic, who is making changes in his life will appear as a Knight also. The idea is that a young-thinking or acting person will be represented by a Knight.

The suit the Knight belongs to will show the character or personality that the Seeker will be expressing in connection with the question asked. This will be qualified by the Knight's upright or reversed position. For example, the Knight of Swords reversed in a woman Seeker's mind placement (attitude towards question asked) would not only indicate a man on a her mind, but would also show her concern about his cruel or prejudiced actions toward her.

If the Knight of Swords reversed appears in her Immediate Future, then he may leave the situation suddenly, or display the qualities we previously mentioned toward the question (prejudice and cruelty), as the next turn of events.

For another example, if the Knight of Wands appears as the cross card, Placement 2, then a young man with qualities of ambition, aggression, positiveness and optimism would be helping the situation at present.

In looking at the Knights we find two basic categories of interpretation. The first and main category is the Knight's character. The second is an occasion or event of consequence coming up in the Seeker's life. Most often you will find that a Knight indicates a person and his character involved in the Seeker's question.

KNIGHT OF WANDS

KNIGHT of WANDS.

The fiery colors of the Knight of Wands indicate his personality and temperament. His character is one of truth and impulse. Outspoken and competitive, ambitious and courageous, he enters a room and makes a definite impression, for he always lets the world know he has arrived! Having strong opinions, he may be easy to argue with, for he enjoys heated discussions and the challenge of winning. You may love him and hate him at the same time, but you can never ignore this Knight and his enthusiasm, spontaneity and joy of life.

The character is open, demonstrative, enjoys people and is probably in a people-oriented profession, outgoing, blunt, humorous and warm. He is an individualist, sports-minded and a creative thinker.

When the Seeker's question does not refer to others, the Knight can simply represent a very important matter emerging in the Seeker's life.

Reversed — This person is selfish, impulsive, argumentative, bossy, jealous, domineering, temperamental and possibly violent, but only if other violence cards are present to confirm this.

He can be overly competitive in addition to being given to abusive, egotistical rages.

If the question is about an event, job problems, unsteady employment, disruptions and unstable circumstances are at work.

KNIGHT OF CUPS

The Knight of Cups is dressed in shades of the blue of his water element. He is more passive and reserved than the Knight of Wands, being basically receptive in nature. Emotive and intuitive, he may enjoy delving into philosophy or psychology. He often helps people and because of his sensitivity he is attuned to their needs. His affinities are for animals, plants, nature or less fortunate, dependent people. He dreams of a Utopian world and may vow to do something to help realize his dream. He must do what he believes in, whether in emotional, material or ambitious matters.

The Knight of Cups is sensitive, idealistic, dreamy, caring and loving. Frequently he is a charmer and knows it. He is usually

KNIGHT of CUPS.

involved with music, either as a musician or dancer or simply with a need for music in his environment; he is also artistic and spiritual.

This card shows qualities of kindness, empathy, romanticism and intelligence.

If the reading is of an event, it is emotional or romantic in nature.

Reversed — The Knight of Cups loses all sincerity and becomes deceptive toward himself and others, living in an escapist world. He prefers his dreams to reality. The lovingness, art and sensitivity toward humanity remain unused and unexpressed.

He is emotionally immature and unreliable. No one should believe everything he says, for he is known to say what he thinks a person wants to hear (flattery) so the person will do what he wants — seduction.

This card shows an escapist unwilling to face reality or responsibility, especially emotionally.

As an event, this card indicates lies and deception.

KNIGHT OF SWORDS

KNIGHT of SWORDS .

A powerful young man moves aggressively through a cloudy, windswept sky. Like a bolt from the blue, this man surprises us by his arrival into our life.

The Knight of Swords enjoys intellectual stimulation. His mental delving and curiosity lead him into a diverse accumulation of interests. Truth, fairness, equality, humanity and his beliefs are important subjects in his life. He may even be involved with a crusade, either personal or professional, where he champions one of these causes.

This Knight leads with his head, not his heart. He can be persuasive and opinionated, strongly insisting he knows what is best.

Mental stimulation is a prerequisite toward involvements, whether oriented to romance, education, friendship or career. He is aggressive and can be sarcastic, cynical or a know-it-all. You'll find him in professions where there are interesting ideas or intellectual excitement, such as law, law enforcement, engineering, economics, technology and communications.

An unexpected, impromptu situation or occurrence is the event.

Reversed — The Knight of Swords' opinions and the forcefulness behind them can become overbearing and pushy. He can become cruel and prejudiced, unfair and brutal — mentally, verbally or physically.

This can be a dictator, a narrow-minded person. The Knight of Swords reversed can view a situation only his way, which is usually filled with misconceptions, prejudices and wrong judgments. From this negative reasoning he arrives at a faulty decision and then vehemently proceeds to make injurious, unreasonable accusations and threats. Sarcasm, cynicism and meanness can be expected.

Sometimes the Knight of Swords upright indicates the quality of suddenness. He pops up in the life suddenly, or a sudden matter can be indicated. In reverse he may suddenly disappear from the Seeker's life. This card reversed can also indicate a situation that suddenly leaves the Seeker's life.

If an event, it is an unheralded leaving of a situation.

KNIGHT OF PENTACLES

KNIGHT of PENTACLES.

The Knight of Pentacles is a practical, dependable, conservative, hardworking man. He works toward security for his life, putting much time, perseverance and patience toward achieving his material goals.

He will share with others if they too contribute time or money toward projects and enterprises. Basically defensive, he loves possessively and gives commitments cautiously and with permanence in mind. Much of life for the Knight of Pentacles is measured in terms of financial value and common sense.

Reliable, stable, cautious and conscientious, he likes routine and the basic comforts in life. He is interested in owning things and making money. The Knight of Pentacles is proud of what he owns rather than what he does. The character often works around industrial complexes, machinery, factories or cars, and is mathematically inclined. He is not a talkative person or openly emotional, so his actions speak louder than his words. His actions are considerate and thoughtful, since he is loyal and responsible.

If an event, the concern is of a job, property or financial matter.

Reversed — The Knight of Pentacles can be unethical, calculating or deceptive concerning money. His sense of proportion about money is lost and he schemes and becomes greedy. On the other hand, he can indicate financial waste; and the inability to hold a job, save money, or provide his own security — general irresponsibility.

If an event, there is instability concerning money, ownership and employment matters.

EXAMPLE INTERPRETATION
Example of interpreting a court card through the placements of a reading using the Page of Wands — Interpretation: Qualities of energy, ambition and drive.

If the Page of Wands appears in the Present (Placement 1), the Seeker is using energy and competing now. If it falls in the second placement of Helps and Obstacles, the Seeker could help their situation by using energy and courage. In the Past (Placement 3 and 4), the Seeker has expressed these qualities of energy and enthusiasm already. In Future placements (5, 6 and 10) enthusiasm and drive may be forthcoming. If this card appears as the Seeker's Attitude (Placement 7), then he or she would be looking at the question with a spirit of enthusiasm, competition, ambition and adventure. The Page of Wands in the Environment position (Placement 8), indicates that others may see the Seeker as outgoing and courageous. If the Page of Wands appears in the Hopes and Fears position (Placement 9), the Seeker would be hoping for those courageous qualities within himself.

If the Page represents a young person involved in the Seeker's question, then the appearance of this card in the mind position (Placement 7) shows the Seeker thinking about the child. If in Placement 8, the Seeker has this child in the Environment. Hopes and Fears about the child and its character or behavior would be indicated by a Page in the ninth position. If the Page falls in the Seeker's Past (Placements 3 and 4), the person's character can be described as it was in the past. This card in the Future placements (5, 6 and 10) reveals the child's future behavior pattern.

You can adjust these interpretations to fit any Court card's character traits and apply them to the appropriate placement. Remember a Page often represents the Seeker himself and the qualities of character he is using to handle the question rather than someone else involved in the reading.

Review of the Pages and Knights

COMPLETION

The Pages

1. List the four ways we interpret the Pages.
   a. _____
   b. _____
   c. _____
   d. _____

2. Which of the four would you use most in interpretation?
   _____.

3. Name three personality traits for adults or children in the Page of Swords.
   a. _____
   b. _____
   c. _____

4. Name three character traits of the Page of Wands.
   a. _____
   b. _____
   c. _____

5. Name three character attributes for both adults and children in the Page of Pentacles.
   a. _____
   b. _____
   c. _____

6. Name three qualities of children and adults personified by the Page of Cups.
   a. _____
   b. _____
   c. _____

7. We can also interpret interests, talents, careers or career potential from the Pages. The Page of _____ is musical, artistic and humanitarian; he loves animals, plants and nature. Often this Page is intuitive, and the development of any of these talents could lead to their use professionally.

8. The Page of _____ is an excellent learner or student at any age. This Page believes life and its experiences are a continual education.

9. Multiple interests occupying both body and mind are attributed to the Page of _____. This Page's talents range from broadcasting, interpreting and journalism to science, the space-age and all technological areas.

10. Energetic and enthusiastic, this Page specializes in performing in various capacities as well as possessing natural leadership abilities. He is the Page of _____.

11. Surprising news brings upset from the Page of _____.

12. A creative, inspirational idea or message is received from the Page of _____.

13. Messages from which we learn something or that bring us information are attributed to the Page of _____.

14. Positive, encouraging news arrives from the Page of _____.

15. The Page of Swords is associated with the special event of _____

16. a. A creative _____that the Seeker wishes to pursue...
    b. is the event indicated by the Page of _____.

17. _____ and _____ are the events depicted in the Page of Pentacles.

18. The colors of
    a. _____ and
    b. _____ in the Page of Cups symbolize the element
    c. _____
    d. How does this relate to the character qualities found in this suit? _____
    _____

19. The Page of Wands wears fire colors to represent his suit and its function of _____.

20. The Swords people, including the Page, wear the colors we see in the sky: whites, yellows, mauves and azure blue. The wind gusts in the scene, indicating _____ and _____.

21. All is still and calm in the serene pasture or field of flowers in the Page of Pentacles. This Page, too, is secure and serene. He values:
    a. _____
    b. _____
    c. _____
    d. How do the colors he wears reinforce this?_____
    _____

The Knights

1. The Tarot Knights have two basic categories of interpretation. These two categories are:
    a. _____
    b. _____

2. The Knights have the most _____ of the Court cards.

3. The Knight of Cups has the qualities of being _____ _____ attributed to his personality.

4. If the Knight of Cups appeared in Placement 2 — Helps and Obstacles, how would these character qualities help the Present situation? Assume the question is about the Seeker only and does not involve others. _____
   _____

5. If another person were asking a question that involved this young man (e.g. a woman and her spouse, a mother concerned about her son), how would you then interpret the Knight of Cups in Placement 2 — Helps and Obstacles?
   _____
   _____

6. The Knight of Pentacles is _____
   _____

7. This card's appearance in the Past or Recent Past placements would indicate: _____
   _____
   _____

8. If the Knight of Pentacles reversed appeared in the Hopes and Fears placement, (Placement 9) it would indicate:
   _____
   _____
   _____

9. The Knight of Swords emerges as the Final Outcome card. What do you, the Reader, do first? _____

_____

_____

10. a. What kind of person is the Knight of Swords?

_____

_____

b. How do we interpret him in Placement ten?

_____

_____

11. The Knight of Wands reversed can be _____

_____

as negative character qualities.

12. Being reversed, what sort of event does this indicate?

_____

_____

13. The Knight of Wands upright in Placement 8 would indicate that others view him as _____

_____ in character.

14. The Page of Swords appears in the Immediate Future placement. What should the Seeker expect?

_____

_____

_____

15. The Page of Pentacles reversed in the Seeker's Possible Future reveals that _____

_____

_____

16. The Page of Cups reversed in the Seeker's Recent Past suggests that_____

_____

_____

17. The Page of Wands reversed falls in the Seeker's Past and Motivation section of the layout, indicating that

_____

_____

_____

MATCHING THE PAGES

Upright Meanings

Personality

_____ 1. Page of Wands	a. Considerate, obedient, careful
_____ 2. Page of Cups	b. Outgoing, friendly, a leader
_____ 3. Page of Swords	c. Sensitive, dreamy, emotional
_____ 4. Page of Pentacles	d. Intelligent, agile, talkative

Messages

_____ 1. Page of Wands	a. Informative message
_____ 2. Page of Cups	b. Intuitive message
_____ 3. Page of Swords	c. Encouraging message
_____ 4. Page of Pentacles	d. Upsetting message

Interests

_____ 1. Page of Wands	a. Education and learning
_____ 2. Page of Cups	b. Communication fields, versatile
_____ 3. Page of Swords	c. Talented, humanitarian or artistic
_____ 4. Page of Pentacles	d. Athletic, competitive

Events

_____ 1. Page of Wands	a. A creative idea contemplated
_____ 2. Page of Cups	b. Spying and suspicious circumstances
_____ 3. Page of Swords	c. Springing forward into adventure
_____ 4. Page of Pentacles	d. Learning and education

Children as Pages

_____ 1. Page of Wands	a. Leads, coaches, performs
_____ 2. Page of Cups	b. Debates, curiously questions
_____ 3. Page of Swords	c. Sings, dances and imagines
_____ 4. Page of Pentacles	d. Devoted student, conscientious and responsible

Reversed Meanings

Personality

_____ 1. Page of Wands
_____ 2. Page of Cups
_____ 3. Page of Swords
_____ 4. Page of Pentacles

a. Rebellious, self-imposed isolation
b. Sharp, sarcastic words; unkind deeds
c. Overdramatic, theatrical behavior
d. Spoiled, lazy, self-indulgent

Character Traits

_____ 1. Page of Wands
_____ 2. Page of Cups
_____ 3. Page of Swords
_____ 4. Page of Pentacles

a. Negative strokes, unhealthy attention-seeking
b. Learning problems, difficulty with authority
c. Talents wasted, world of illusion or escapism
d. Sly, tricky, fickle

Messages

_____ 1. Page of Wands
_____ 2. Page of Cups
_____ 3. Page of Swords
_____ 4. Page of Pentacles

a. Heartbreaking, upsetting news
b. Uninspiring, unencouraging message
c. Upsetting news; falseness is revealed
d. Refusal to heed informative messages

MATCHING THE KNIGHTS
Upright Meanings
Job Fields

_____ 1. Involved with writing, journalism, or communication fields. Could be a legal representative or law enforcer.

a. Knight of Wands
b. Knight of Cups
c. Knight of Swords
d. Knight of Pentacles

_____ 2. Salesperson; competitive, adventurous, challenging types of employment.

_____ 3. Works in mechanical, technical fields or around machinery. Handles money at work.

_____ 4. Emotionally involved with his work, often involved with humanitarian ventures or artistic jobs.

Romance

_____ 1. Intellectual stimulus intrigues this Knight toward becoming emotionally involved. Liberated and fair toward others.

a. Knight of Wands
b. Knight of Cups
c. Knight of Swords
d. Knight of Pentacles

_____ 2. Loving and giving by nature. is idealistic, romantic and sincere.

_____ 3. Expresses feeling by actions and thoughtful deeds. Is defensive. A devoted, possessive lover.

_____ 4. Includes his loved ones in all of his adventures. Encouraging, friendly, generous lover.

General Attributes

_____ 1. Enjoys outdoors. Rugged, nature-loving, financially astute, hard-working, stable and quiet.

_____ 2. Music-loving, drawn to water for solace or recreation. Philosophic, intuitive, meditative.

_____ 3. Athletic, egotistical, personable, pioneering. A leader or traveler.

_____ 4. Avid reader, campaigner, crusader, debater, conversationalist. Believes in the power of the mind and psychology. Interested in politics, the economy and human rights.

a. Knight of Wands
b. Knight of Cups
c. Knight of Swords
d. Knight of Pentacles

Events

_____ 1. Knight of Wands
_____ 2. Knight of Cups
_____ 3. Knight of Swords
_____ 4. Knight of Pentacles

a. Event concerning a property, financial or employment matter.
b. Event of an unexpected or sudden departure.
c. Event concerned with the feeling aspect of life.
d. Event of a dramatic adventure. An important event.

Reversed Meanings

_____ 1. Jealous, argumentative, possibly violent.

_____ 2. Deceives himself and others. A seducer.

_____ 3. Prejudiced accusations, unfair threats.

_____ 4. Poor work and spending habits. Is overly possessive.

a. Knight of Wands
b. Knight of Cups
c. Knight of Swords
d. Knight of Pentacles

Answers to Review of the Pages and Knights

COMPLETION

The Pages

1. a. A child and his or her character.
   b. The character of someone involved in the Seeker's question, or the Seeker's personality expressed in the question.
   c. Messages
   d. Events.
2. People and their personality traits.
3. Any of the following character traits can be for the Page of Swords: cleverness, intelligence, communication ability, agility, diplomacy, adaptability, curiosity and flexibility.
4. Character traits of the Page of Wands are leadership, courage, competitiveness, athletic ability, ambition, impulsive, magnanimity, innovation and love of attention. He or she is enthusiastic, energetic, personable, outgoing and giving.
5. Page of Pentacles characters are responsible, respectful, broad-minded, patient, careful, cautious, timid, conforming and respectful of authority.
6. Persons characterized by the Page of Cups are dreamy, poetic, romantic, idealistic, psychic, artistic, sympathetic, emotional, kind, humanitarian and considerate.
7. Cups.
8. Pentacles.
9. Swords.
10. Wands.
11. Swords.
12. Cups.
13. Pentacles.
14. Wands.
15. Spying.
16. a. idea
    b Cups
17. a. Studying
    b. education, learning, training.
18. a. blue
    b. green
    c. water

    d. water colors of blue and green symbolize the quality of flowing movement, suggestive of emotionalism, responsiveness and intuition, all aspects within ourselves that we flow with.

19. Desire, drive, courage, energy and enthusiasm — all qualities we are said to "burn" with.

20. The wind indicates stirring or exciting of activities that stimulate this Page's mind, body and actions.

21. a. stability
    b. responsibility
    c. practicality, reality or money.
    d. His colors are down-to-earth shades of brown and nature's green.

The Knights

1. a. The personality or character of a young man involved in the reading.
   b. An occasion or event of consequence emerging in the Seeker's life.
2. Power, influence, significance.
3. Emotional, loving, sensitive, idealistic, dreamy, kind, intelligent, empathetic.
4. He could help the situation by expressing his qualities of kindness, empathy, sensitivity and so on in relation to his question.
5. The Knight is a young man involved in the Seeker's question. He may be applying his character traits of sensitivity and kindness to help the Seeker.

   Note: If the First Placement card indicates presently upsetting and unsettled conditions, then the Seeker may be upset about this Knight and is now questioning his character. In this case he would be the Obstacle rather than the Helping force.
6. Reliable, stable, cautious, conscientious, materialistic, loyal and responsible.
7. He has applied these qualities in the past. If it fell in the Foundation (Placement 4, Past/Motivation) then he may be motivated by this past to ask his present question.
8. It indicates that he himself or the person asking a question about him is fearful of his being careless and unethical or deceptive about money matters. There are fears of financial insecurity or job instability.
9. First you lay out the next card, the eleventh card. Because the Knight is a person affecting or determining the outcome of the Seeker's question and the following card reveals what he will be doing or how he will affect the Seeker's future.
10. a. Strong-minded, opinionated, aggressive, headstrong. He enters the Seeker's life suddenly.
    b. This indicates that the outcome of the Seeker's question will be determined by a man who possesses these character traits. The card following the Knight of Swords would reveal what he was going to do in the Seeker's future or how he will affect the outcome of the situation.
11. Jealous, over-competitive, temperamental, egotistical, raging and selfish.
12. Employment disturbances.

13. Ambitious, energetic, competitive, open, warm, giving and personable.
14. Expect the unexpected: upsetting news, unstable conditions. Warn the Seeker to be alert for such a possibility and to apply tact and diplomacy when necessary in dealing with the event. The Seeker may also be spied on or dealt with suspiciously.
15. Possibly in the Future the Seeker will feel misunderstood and isolated. He or she may balk at an authority figure or rules and regulations. The Seeker may even make a repeated mistake by refusing to learn from prior ones. Carelessness and irresponsible behavior could manifest.
16. Recently he or she has felt very lazy and uninspired. Listless and indolent, the Seeker may have chosen a dreamy fantasy world instead of coping with realities. Talents have atrophied and inspiration is lacking.
17. In the past, the Seeker was temperamental, hurt and unstable. Sadly, the Seeker's overwhelming need for love and attention caused troublesome circumstances. Previously, this Page was theatrical and overdramatized conditions to gain attention. Now the person may be concerned about repeating this Page's behavior and, is motivated to ask the present question because of these past self-destructive activities.

MATCHING THE PAGES
Upright Meanings

Personality
1. **b**   2. **c**   3. **d**   4. **a**

Messages
1. **c**   2. **b**   3. **d**   4. **a**

Interests
1. **d**   2. **c**   3. **b**   4. **a**

Events
1. **c**   2. **a**   3. **b**   4. **d**

Children
1. **a**   2. **c**   3. **b**   4. **d**

Reversed Meanings

Personality
1. **c**   2. **d**   3. **b**   4. **a**

Character Traits
1. **a**   2. **c**   3. **d**   4. **b**

Messages
1. **a**   2. **b**   3. **c**   4. **d**

MATCHING THE KNIGHTS
Upright Meanings

Job Fields

1. c   2. a   3. d   4. b

Romance

1. c   2. b   3. d   4. a

General Attributes

1. d   2. b   3. a   4. c

Events

1. d   2. c   3. b   4. a

Reversed Meanings

1. a   2. b   3. c   4. d

Assignment

(See Lesson 12)

THE COURT CARDS — QUEENS AND KINGS

The Queens

Queens are women over 18 years of age. They always represent females or the Seeker's character qualities expressed in approaching the question.

See Lesson 1 on Court Cards for further interpretation information.

QUEEN OF WANDS

QUEEN of WANDS.

Representative of all three fire signs, this Queen has a particular affinity for Leo, as suggested by the lions decorating her throne. Also belonging to the feline family is the black cat at the Queen's feet. In astrology, we have the leonine Leos who enjoy attention, rulership and being Queen or King of their particular jungle, be it their career, domestic or social life. The cat Leo is a quieter type of person who also loves adventure and independence but achieves this in more private or subtler ways.

Gold for the sign Leo and the sun is the color of the Queen's gown. Both the gold coloring and the sunflower she holds suggest spiritual awareness and an open, compassionate heart. Attractive and majestic, intelligent and ambitious, no wonder this Queen commands attention!

As with the other Wands Court cards, people respond to this woman. She exudes honesty and warmth as well as competency.

The Queen of Wands is a happy, positive, sunny card, much like the disposition attributed to her. Because she belongs to the suit of Wands, we can expect a courageous, adventurous spirit and an ambitious, enterprising nature.

Creative with strong ideas, this woman asserts herself for a cause. Frequently, career is her motivation. She also will be involved in social conditions, politics, campaigning, personal self-expression, performing, sports, creativity and self-growth through self-discovery.

Intensely and joyfully involved with all she creates, she participates also in family and domestic decision-making. Nature is one of her many loves, as are drama, independence, self-expression and learning. Confidently and with foresight, she courageously accomplishes her many goals.

Creative, resourceful, positive, popular, she knows how to give as well as take. She has a sense of authority and power and can influence people and her surroundings. She is often found as a leader within home, family, groups, organizations or career. She knows how to "catch flies with honey," using her feminine charm and beauty to influence others.

This woman enjoys healthy competition and approaches life with an adventurous spirit. She possesses strong personal feelings concerning subjects important to her.

Reversed — One of the striking features about the Queen of Wands reveresed is the negativity associated with her black cat. This symbol represents seduction and deception. This Queen, when reversed, turns on her charm and sexuality, using it to force her way to her goals and ambitions. Her desires can now be ruthlessly competitive, egotistical and vengeful. Jealousy, greed and envy often motivate her subtle or bullying attacks upon other people. Unchecked ambition can drive her relentlessly forward on a campaign of ruin and destructiveness.

In a milder form, the Queen of Wands reversed can be a pushy, narrow-minded person, subject to telling lies and accomplishing goals through devious methods.

She can be a selfish, egotistical manipulator, overly ambitious and execessively domineering. She uses her sexuality craftily to influence others, twist information and exaggerate situations with bravado, creating deliberately deceptive conditions. Her mottoes are "Me first," and "My way."

QUEEN OF CUPS

QUEEN of CUPS.

The symbols of water, the color blue and the beach where the tide rolls in, suggest the habitat of the Queen of Cups. Water takes the shape of its container. The idea here is that the Queen of Cup's sensitivity and emotional nature are so prominent, that often she becomes absorbed in and molded by her surroundings. She assumes the moods and feelings of others, hurts where they hurt, rejoices when they rejoice. If support is needed, she's there; if understanding is necessary, she intuitively senses it and responds. Often she is prophetic about those close to her and their lives.

The Queen of Cups loves harmony and peace. Unlike the Queen of Wands who searches for adventure and life's excitement, this Queen treasures tranquility and the time to dream, imagine and contemplate. Her environment is decorated with mementos of friends and family, for she cherishes remembrances of those whom she loves.

Love in general plays a strong role in her life in which much time and effort are devoted to the needs of those she cares about. Emotional and intuitive, this Queen often senses the feelings of her loved ones, and takes great satisfaction in providing the support and comfort that those around her require. Her life is often geared toward fulfilling others while her dreams remain locked up inside her, perhaps someday to be fulfilled.

When her dreams are expressed they are of a creative nature: art, music, poetry, writing and all related creative fields. Psychic sensitivity and intuition are strong within her and she may pursue goals of discovering this powerful subconscious part of herself. The occult, psychology, philosophy, religion and mysticism are her interests.

Facing the sea with her throne perched along the shoreline, she dwells on the edge of the powerful imaginative, psychic and subconscious depths and can dip into these forces at will.

Her lovingness is total and devoted. It soothes and calms like a warm wave of affection. Excessive sensitivity makes her vulnerable to fluctuating moods and imagined rejection.

When this woman ventures into the world, she finds it difficult to relate to others without becoming overly sensitive and psychically vulnerable. Perhaps this is the reason why she retreats into the safety of her home and limits her empathetic giving to her close friends and family members. Otherwise she is too subject to the vibrations she perceives from others; her emotions would be in continual turbulence if she were constantly open and responding to people.

This Queen is sensitive, sympathetic, emotional and imaginative, and often has a love of music, poetry, literature and arts, as well as dedication to home and family.

Reversed — The oversensitivity can become unbearable. The Queen of Cups reversed sacrifices herself for others, becoming insecure or emotionally weak, resentful and vulnerable. She seeks to escape these problems that her emotionalism and need for acceptance have brought her. Confused and indecisive, she steps into an escapist kind of world filled with illusions and unrealistic dreaming and fantasy. Perhaps alcohol or drugs keep her there, or her own fears have brought her to this tiny, unrealistic universe. Morbid worries interfere with her psychic aptitude; dreams frighten and haunt her. Daydreams are negative imaginings of the worst possible events. she is unable to forget and release the unhappy past. When the Queen of Cups appears reversed, it represents a woman who can be emotionally unbalanced. Her judgments can be wrong, fearful and unrealistic. Reality escapes her and she seeks to escape reality. Her personal emotional problems take her on a tidal wave of ups and downs, drowning her in emotional confusion!

She needs to lead with her head, not her heart, and apply discipline. The Queen of Cups reversed must learn to be objective rather than interpreting everyone and everything in her life as personally for or against her.

QUEEN OF SWORDS

This Queen's facial features are sharply defined, denoting a keen mind and action with intent. Birds, clouds, slyphs and butterflies symbolize the powerful mental abilities attributed to the element air. Her firm grasp of the Sword suggests her understanding of these energies and the correct use of their powers.

A Victorian mourning bracelet is prominently displayed on her wrist, telling us of past hurts, losses and grief.

The Queen of Swords is strong; the quality of self-rulership is attributed to her. At one time the traditional interpretation of this queen was a woman suffering; loneliness and the loss of loved ones. Sorrows beset her and her life was filled with grief.

QUEEN OF SWORDS.

Today we view the Queen of Swords from a different perspective. Her aloneness does not indicate loneliness; instead, it suggests independence.

A woman may be married or otherwise attached and still be represented by the Queen of Swords, indicating that she is self-reliant and on her own to a large extent within the relationship's tie. Freely, individually, autonomously, she rules her life.

Because she belongs to the Swords suit, her intellect is highlighted. She is strongly opinionated, analytical, and mentally astute. She has a quick, intense and versatile intelligence which she uses to make fair and well-thought-out decisions.

Her head rules over her heart. She analyzes her feelings and keeps her emotions checked, Gently but firmly she counsels and guides those around her. Her unique ability to view both sides of a situation with depth provides her with the advantage of mental clarity and accurate judgments.

Learning and mental pursuits attract this Queen. She is interested in the powers of the mind and its inner psychological workings.

She can analyze and define, direct and concentrate, discipline and aggressively persevere toward her goals and beliefs. Her motivations are toward action, experiencing life, participation in educational accomplishments and achieving personal liberty.

Her mind is her weapon in the battlefield of life. It can be sharp and critical, perceptive and analytical.

She may have experienced difficulties, set-backs and life's problems. Her image is a powerful one, revealing that she has overcome her obstacles and risen above her enemies, who may be others in her life or her own emotional, physical and mental self.

Fairness, equality, liberation, humanity and education are her causes. The communication fields, from speaking and journalism to technology and teaching, are other areas of interest designated to this Queen.

Reversed — Misery loves company, and the Queen of Swords reversed fills you in on all the bad news and gossip. This Queen informs you of her opinions — which are inevitably negative, suspicious and discouraging — regardless whether you've asked for her viewpoint or not.

The trademark of the Queen of Swords reversed is her insistence on living in the past. Usually an unhappy memory haunts her and she refuses to bury this painful past incident. Bitterly, she drags her unhappy past into her present as if to wear her misery as a shield of self-defense, using it as an excuse not to exert herself toward growth. She darkens her present and poisons the future of those who come under her influence and her domain.

In reverse, her sword of victory becomes a weapon for retaliation and revenge. Still mentally active, she turns her mind to cunning and manufactures manipulative, devious plans. Her words can be cruel, her judgments prejudiced and excessively harsh, and she may use her cold accusations as her defense.

The hardships life has handed her have become too overwhelming. She develops a chip on her shoulder and becomes unhappy. Her opinions may be one-sided, misinformed and not to be trusted.

This card carries qualities of prejudice, self-pity, deception, back-stabbing, and poor decision-making.

QUEEN OF PENTACLES

QUEEN of PENTACLES

The Queen of Pentacles is enthroned outdoors in the fertile abundance of her environment. This woodland picture teems with flora and fauna, suggesting prosperous results from her prolific energies. This is a woman who communes with nature and is innately productive and creative. Business, property, possessions and monies succeed and flourish under her domain.

Cautious, conservative, wise and practical, the Queen of Pentacles is trustworthy and emotionally mature.

Because she reigns in the suit of Pentacles, this Queen values security and stability, preferably of her own making. Similar to the other Pentacle Court cards, she is steadfast and persevering when it comes to achieving her goal of financial independence.

Often these women are steadily employed and career-minded, willing to work hard for the luxuries, security and personal independence they cherish. Ownership of valuables, property and companies are part of the Queen of Pentacles' intentions.

This earth Queen personifies the traditional associations of finances and employment with the Pentacles suit. She also holds the realistic, practical attributes belonging to the Pentacles and the qualities of creativity and love of nature.

Creating a beautiful environment is one of her many abilities. Her ideas are constructive and well-organized. She tends toward possessiveness with loved ones and is willing to invest time, energy and even money in helping others become secure.

In her estimation, responsibility is what life is all about. She realizes that through the acceptance of it she will achieve the financial rewards and esteemed reputation she so richly deserves.

The Queen indicates a creative woman who contributes care, reason and imagination. Her home is important to her and she expresses her creativity there as well as in business, work, family and nature.

This Queen needs to develop security within herself rather than relying on her possessions to give her comfort and stability. She is confident, realistic, and practical.

Reversed — The Queen of Pentacles reversed may be insecure and unsure of herself. In the reversed position her creativity remains stagnant and she has little financial power or independence. Reliance on others to make decisions for her has brought her to a very precarious and unstable position. She broods, becomes moody, blames others for her problems. Stubbornly she refuses to assume responsibility for her own life and actions. Her preference is to live her life for and through others, relying on them to direct her thoughts and actions.

She may be insecure and lack confidence. She doesn't bother with herself or her home's appearance and becomes noncommittal and untrustworthy. Her skills are unused. She is sad and pensive, weak-willed and vacillating. She wavers in life's affairs.

The Kings

The Kings depict men who have matured, settled and achieved a position in life.

The rules for the Kings are the same as for the Queens: the Kings are people or aspects of people's characters.

There is one exception to this: the King of Swords reversed indicates an event which might be unfair, a decision prejudiced against the Seeker.

KING OF WANDS

KING of WANDS

The King of Wands is a creative, enterprising person who always needs a situation to challenge him or an ambitious goal to excite him. He takes pleasure in healthy competition in the games of business, politics, athletics, and gains attention by staging lively arguments, heated debates and laughing, joking and teasing.

The King of Wands has finally reached his ambitious career goals and may now turn to a world where others need his assistance.

Basically a warm, generous character, he becomes involved with service clubs and humanitarian organizations, contributing his commanding and effective presence to help, advertise, organize and accomplish goals.

Perhaps he has been overly ambitious and self-involved; now that he has achieved success, he feels the need to do some giving or caring to benefit others.

He believes that life is a stage and he aspires toward a starring role in the performance. Self-starting and ambitious, he prefers to work independently as his own boss.

Above all, life for this King is to be lived and experienced. With joy and anticipation, he plunges continually into new enterprises, relishing the excitement of participation and adventure. Courageous and friendly, he enjoys the outdoors, people, sports and competition. He is husband and family man, involved in politics, community action or groups and organizations. In his career he uses his natural decisiveness, charisma and foresight as a leader, manager or administrator.

Honesty, generosity and trustworthiness are his character traits.

Reversed — The King of Wands in reversed position has lost his friendly, generous qualities. Selfishness, righteous demands and mercenary tactics may now dominate his once open and sharing personality.

Perhaps his arrogance has created a "little empire" for this self-serving individual, to the exclusion of all persons, places and things not adhering to his ruling policies.

He grows suspicious, closing and confining his world to his own self-seeking goals and egotistical gratification.

"I want everything done now and my way," declares the King of Wands reversed. Antagonistic, he may be ready for a dispute to enforce his demands.

He could be temperamental and severe, prejudiced and narrow-minded. Argumentative, domineering, selfishly wanting his own way, he is bossy yet dislikes being told what to do.

KING OF CUPS

KING of CUPS.

The King of Cups has a deep understanding of life and its inner psychological and spiritual meaning. He applies his intense intelligence into probing the depth of the soul.

Whatever this King may be involved in, his purpose is always deeply sincere. The water rolling in waves through the card indicates the emotional powers of this King, stirring him to meaningful action.

His position in life may be one of creative fields or the arts. Medicine, law, counseling and business are major areas of interest. His resoluteness and moral courage motivate him with emotional energy and purpose to feel strongly about the beliefs in which he becomes involved. He possesses powerful subconscious powers of intuition, imagination and creativity.

On first encounter with this King, you may not realize the intensity behind his passionate yet well-controlled, quiet and intellectual self-presentation. As you come to know him further, his deep feelings and profound caring become evident. He feels genuine concern for people, loved ones and social conditions. This part of his character emerges gradually and people's admiration for him becomes great respect.

Responsible and caring, genuine and compassionate, he is like a treasure recovered from the depth of his element, the unfathomable sea.

He enjoys artistic, philosophical, psychological and scientific pursuits.

This person can be a legal or medical advisor, or a counselor.

Reversed — The King of Cups reversed is emotionally immature. Having never come to terms with his feelings, he may appear defensive, sarcastic and neurotic. Sensitivity problems abound as he drowns his agitation in pursuit of a variety of illusions. He lies to himself about his feelings and may reinforce this self-deception with the use of alcohol, drugs, sexual escapades and senseless, meaningless pursuits of a deluded nature.

When reversed, he can be untrustworthy and his advice may be inaccurate. His words are insincere and may be calculated to manipulate and deceive others to his own advantage.

Emotional problems, when buried in the subconscious can create some serious unhealthy dependencies. Frightened and threatened by his own sensitivity, he may conceal his insecurity by presenting a distant or uncaring facade. Other manifestations of this King's personality problems are weakness and ineffectualness, which he may or may not conceal with an outer show of hostility.

KING OF SWORDS

KING of SWORDS.

The King of Swords does not have the aloneness and sorrow of his consort, the Queen of Swords. Belonging to the Swords, he has fought mental or physical battles. Life has handed him hardships, either personal or professional, and he has conquered them. Because of his struggles in life, he can base his judgments on his own personal experience.

He has matured since we last saw him as a Knight, having achieved success in some of his ambitious, youthful goals. Challenges have been met and conquered; wisdom and discrimination have been gained.

Being a decision-maker, the King of Swords listens carefully and weighs cautiously all conclusions he is required to make. He blends honesty with diplomacy and impartiality with empathy, producing decisions that are fair.

In a reading, he represents a decision that will be fairly rendered over the Seeker.

The King of Swords is a professional man, often a lawyer, doctor or educator. He may be involved with a job where he receives recognition for specialized skills or administrative work — a specialist. Often he has a position in life (career, home, society) where he is the decision-maker or arbitrator.

Intellectual by nature, he will discuss topics of humanitarian, philosophical or global importance. This King has very strong beliefs and yet is willing to listen to other sides of a debate to ensure fairness is received on all sides.

His kindness is expressed through his actions, words and deeds. This King has faith in the power of the written or spoken word.

He keeps his feelings to himself, preferring to discuss issues of an impersonal nature (e.g., economics, government, world conditions and politics).

Reversed — The King of Swords brings an unfair verdict that may negatively affect the Seeker.

Prejudiced and filled with malice, this King reversed seeks revenge indiscriminately. Woe to the innocent bystander who incurs his wrath. He acts with vengeance, attempting to annihilate completely those who oppose him.

The world may appear a battleground to this reversed King. He takes up his sword and fights real and imagined battles often fabricated in his own mind.

His skillful cleverness turns to devious dreams. He plots, blames, schemes, and fiercely executes his accusations.

Legal difficulties may also be indicated by this King in reverse.

The King of Swords loses his balance and tumbles into prejudiced thinking and unjust attitudes. His quiet personality turns cold and ruthless. His comments are cynical and filled with suspicion.

KING OF PENTACLES

We find the King of Pentacles seated amidst his possessions and wealth. His hard work and perseverance have paid off richly. He now is at a stage in his life where he can pause to reflect on his large accumulations. This King has achieved much in the financial area of life, involving investments, buying and selling, property and land deals, business or agriculture ventures. He has the unique ability to look at the land and see what vast potentials are quietly lying within its depth. He loves the earth and has a great feel for nature. Because of his kinship with the earth, he creates a bountiful harvest from nature's yield.

KING of PENTACLES.

To this King, "Money talks." He knows how to spend, profit

and "wheel and deal." Often he measures others' importance to him by their financial worth. To the King of Pentacles, it's what you own, not how you think, that counts.

He is a great financier, but he also has excellent mechanical and engineering skills.

Being a practical King, he believes in what his senses tell him and is doubtful about anything he can't see, touch, hear, taste or smell.

Often this man comes from a traditional, conservative background. He is especially old-fashioned regarding his family. Possessiveness of loved ones is a downfall for him. Stubbornly he demands respect and loyalty. He heralds his ancestry and responds deeply to his past.

He is basically a cautious man, but will take chances for material gain.

The Knight of Pentacles has matured; now as the King, he finds his serious commitment to work and to establishing himself have paid off.

Spending and gifts are still his way of showing affection and love.

Reversed — The King of Pentacles reversed can be an obstinate, bullying man. He may be completely materialistic and willing to do anything for money.

He worships materialism and will turn to illegal, unethical means to gain wealth and position. He is impressed by people's status and social position and has developed a highly inflated ego in attempting to develop the same prestige for himself.

His monetary dealings are not to be trusted. If his money isn't dirty, then his methods may be.

In reverse this King is stubborn and impractical. His expectations of his loved ones are extreme. Tradition becomes a dictatorship within his bigoted, totalitarian leadership.

This card may indicate a workaholic or, on the other hand, an idle, lazy man.

This man labors in vain as a slave to prestige or materialism. He has a bad financial reputation, is devious and may be fraudulent with his financial schemes.
He may use his money to influence, buy or entice others into doing his bidding.

When reversed, the King of Pentacles cares only for his possessions, and may ignore his loved ones and even his own mental, emotional and spiritual needs.

Qualities of stubbornness and inflexibility are indicated.

Review of the Queens and Kings

COMPLETION

1. Name three major character qualities of the Queen and King of Wands.
   a. _____
   b. _____
   c. _____

2. The Queen and King of Swords both have the main Swords qualities of:
   a. _____
   b. _____
   c. _____

3. The Pentacles King and Queen can be described as:
   a. _____
   b. _____
   c. _____

4. Three major qualities associated with the King and Queen of Cups are:
   a. _____
   b. _____
   c. _____

5. The King of _____ believes strongly in fairness and equality and that there is power in the written and spoken word.

6. The Queen of _____ often retreats because of her sensitivity to her surroundings.

7. The King of _____ believes it's what a man owns and works for that is important.

8. The Queen of _____ reversed is dominating and uses her attractiveness to her advantage.

9. The King of _____ reversed has serious difficulties in facing his emotional nature.

10. The Queen of _____ reversed bitterly drags her unhappy past into her present.

11. The King of _____ believes that life is a challenge to be enjoyed.

12. The Queen of _____ reversed is unstable and overly dependent on others.

13. The King of Pentacles reversed cares more about:
    a. _____ than humanity.

b. He is _____ and

c. manipulates money _____

14. The Queen of Cups reversed prefers to live in a:

    a. _____ world filled with

    b. _____ and

    c. _____ fears.

15. The Queen of Wands is _____ and _____ minded.

16. The King of Swords reversed is:

    a. _____, _____ and

    b. _____ judges and makes accusations.

17. The King of Cups is interested in:

    a. _____

    b. _____ and

    c. _____

18. The Queen of Swords is _____ rather than lonely.

19. The King of Wands reversed is _____ and _____ wanting all his own way.

20. The Queen of Pentacles communes with:

    a. _____ and believes in having her own

    b. _____

MATCHING THE QUEENS
Upright Meanings

_____ 1. Values financial security and independence. Works at becoming her own source of stability.

_____ 2. Attractive, popular, with leadership ability.

_____ 3. Strongly intelligent, decisive and perceptive.

_____ 4. Sentimental, sensitive, intuitive, loving.

a. Queen of Wands
b. Queen of Cups
c. Queen of Swords
d. Queen of Pentacles

Reversed Meanings

____ 1. Cruel words, unfair judgments, bitterness.

____ 2. Vulnerable emotionally; frightened imaginings.

____ 3. Turns on the charm to win favors.

____ 4. Unstable; insecurity produces psychological imbalance.

a. Queen of Wands
b. Queen of Cups
c. Queen of Swords
d. Queen of Pentacles

MATCHING THE KINGS
Upright Meanings

____ 1. Sincere. Empathetic advisor, kind and deep. "I believe."

____ 2. Aggressive, has popularity and prestige. Friendly. "The world is a stage."

____ 3. Decision-maker, fair, intelligent and highly ethical. "Power is in the mind."

____ 4. Accumulates financial security, valuable possessions and holdings. "Money talks."

a. King of Wands
b. King of Cups
c. King of Swords
d. King of Pentacles

Reversed Meanings

____ 1. Argumentative, selfish, domineering.

____ 2. Emotionally disturbed and neurotic.

____ 3. Gambler, financial manipulator, untrustworthy.

____ 4. Inaccurate outlook, unfair judgments.

a. King of Wands
b. King of Cups
c. King of Swords
d. King of Pentacles

Answers to Review of the Queens and Kings

COMPLETION

1. a. Friendly, people-loving,
   b. Ambitious, open, leaderlike
   c. Adventurous.
2. a. Intelligence
   b. Decision-making
   c. Fair-mindedness
3. a. Security-conscious
   b. Money-minded
   c. Earth or nature-loving
4. a. Sensitivity
   b. Emotionalism
   c. Depth of feeling
5. King of Swords
6. Queen of Cups
7. King of Pentacles
8. Queen of Wands reversed
9. King of Cups reversed
10. Queen of Swords reversed
11. King of Wands
12. Queen of Pentacles
13. a. Money
    b. Stubborn
    c. Unethically
14. a. Dream or fantasy
    b. Illusions
    c. Morbid
15. Ambitious and career
16. a. Revengeful, malicious
    b. Unfairly
17. a. Psychology
    b. Philosophy
    c. The arts
18. Independent or self-sufficient
19. Selfish and demanding
20. a. Nature
    b. Security

MATCHING THE QUEENS
Upright Meanings
1. **d**   2. **a**   3. **c**   4. **b**

Reversed Meanings
1. **c**   2. **b**   3. **a**   4. **d**

MATCHING THE KINGS
Upright Meanings
1. **b**   2. **a**   3. **c**   4. **d**

Reversed Meanings
1. **a**   2. **b**   3. **d**   4. **c**

Assignment

(See Lesson 12)

ASSIGNMENT FOR THE PAGES, KNIGHTS, QUEENS AND KINGS

We are using the Minor Arcana plus the Court Cards, therefore, general observations may be made.

THE INDICATOR
Indicator card — Queen of Cups

THE CUT
Past — Page of Wands
Present is the — Ten of Cups
The Future — Seven of Pentacles reversed

THE READING

Placement 1	Present Influence — Eight of Cups reversed
Placement 2	Helps and Obstacles — Knight of Cups
Placement 3	Past, Motivation — Knight of Wands reversed
Placement 4	Recent Past — Seven of Swords reversed
Placement 5	Possible Outcome — Ten of Swords reversed
Placement 6	Immediate Future — Page of Swords
Placement 7	Seeker's Attitude — Nine of Wands
Placement 8	Others' Viewpoint — King of Swords reversed
Placement 9	Hopes and Fears — Ace of Cups
Placement 10	Final Outcome — Six of Cups reversed

Your first observations in looking over the layout indicate some general trends contained in the reading.

1. The strongest suit, including the Indicator, is:
   a. _____ indicating
   b. _____.

2. a. The other dominant suit is:
   a. _____, suggesting
   b. _____.

3. a. There are _____ Court cards.
   b. Do they all represent other people involved in the reading? _____
   c. If not, what would their appearance indicate?
   _____

4. Another important factor is a predominance of inverted or reversed cards.
   a. How many cards are reversed in the reading, excluding the Cut? _____
   b. What does this suggest? _____

5. a. The Present Cut indicates _____
   b. She experienced _____
   in the past in relation to her question.
   c. Her future indicates _____
   represented by the Seven of Pentacles in reverse.

6. Describe the Queen of Cups.
   _____
   _____

7. What aspect of life is she inquiring about?
   _____

8. The Eight of Cups reversed indicates:
   _____
   (assuming the Seeker has confirmed that others are involved with the question.)

9. The Knight of Cups is in the second position of Helps and Obstacles. This is a young man of _____ character.

10. Because he appears in the Helps or Obstacles placement, he may be:
    a. _____ the Seeker. The Seeker may also be questioning someone's character or involvement when a Court card appears in this placement.

    b. In considering the Knight of Cups' position and character, what would the Queen of Cups be questioning about him? _____

11. The Past is the Knight of Wands reversed. Describe his character and who he could be.

_____

12. The Seven of Swords reversed in the Seeker's Recent Past suggests that recently _____

_____

13. The Possible Future holds the Ten of Swords reversed. What could the Future hold for the Queen of Cups?

_____

14. The Page of Swords indicates the next event that will occur.
    a. What will this event be? _____
    b. What character qualities should be applied in handling this upcoming event? _____
    c. What must the Queen of Cups be prepared for?

_____

15. The Queen's attitude is the Nine of Wands. Therefore, her outlook is _____

16. The King of Swords reversed is in her Environment (Others' Viewpoints), indicating that _____

_____

17. In the Hopes and Fears position is the Ace of Cups. Interpret:_____

_____

18. The Six of Cups reversed indicates:

_____

for her future in this situation.

Answers for Assignment
Using Pages, Knights, Queens and Kings

General observations in judging a reading excluding the Cut.

1. a. Cups
   b. Loved ones or an emotional question.
2. a. Swords
   b. Difficulties and conditions of strife. The Seeker may be doing some serious questioning and thinking about an emotional (referring to the Cups) matter.
3. a. Four (not including the Indicator Card).
   b. No, not all of this reading's Court cards are separate people. The majority of the Court cards are other people; the exceptions are the Pages.
   c. The Pages are messages or character qualities the Seeker will be expressing toward the question.
4. a. There are six reversed cards.
   b. Some amount of upset about her question. Note that they are evenly dispersed between past, present and future placements.
5. a. Currently she feels content and **satisfied with a relationship or family situation**. We use the emotional meanings of the Ten of Cups because she has chosen the Queen as her Indicator card.
   b. The Page of Wands indicates that she **experienced dynamic, encouraging and courageous energy** regarding the past of her question. Perhaps her relationship brought these qualities into her life, like a new birth or a springtime situation. The Page may also be a child who is important to her. Use character traits to determine who this Page is.
   c. In her future she may encounter a **time of soul-searching and reevaluation**. Perhaps money worries will also occur in her future.
6. The Queen of Cups is a **sensitive, emotional, loving woman**.
7. She has asked about an emotional topic, or she is sensitive and emotional about her question.
8. **Enjoyment of social times** and that her present life is filled with ease.

9. The Knight of Cups is a **sincere, sensitive, emotional, young man**.

10. a. Helping
    b. She may be questioning his emotional sincerity and intentions.
    Note: The Eight of Cups reversed suggests that she is not having present difficulties. The Ten of Cups in her Present Cut reinforces her present happy state. His intentions may be under her scrutiny but not because of dire relationship problems.

11. Influencing her life in the past was a young man between 18 and 35 who was argumentative, jealous and overly aggressive. He may have been a past loved one. Because he appears in the Seeker's Past/ Motivation section of the reading, she may be motivated to ask her present question about the Knight of Cups and his character. Her past held a difficult, disturbing young man with whom she contended. She **bases her present concern on this prior conflict**.

12. She has received **an apology or statement of appreciation from an unexpected source**. Also, she may have decided recently to be her own best friend and to help herself achieve a positive, happy and productive life. This is supported by the Page of Wands in the Past Cut placement.

13. The Queen of Cups could find difficulties and concerns lifting and being relieved.

14. a. **An upsetting message containing surprising information. An event of a suspicious or spying nature**. Perhaps she will soon receive an unexpected, surprising message from an observer informing her of questionable, irregular circumstances connected with the question she has asked. She may hear from or about the Knight of Wands in her Past.
    b. The Page of Swords also indicates character qualities in handling this unusual message. The qualities applied are those of **diplomacy, adaptability, agility, flexibility and openness in talking and communicating**.
    c. **Prepare to expect the upsetting message** and to be communicative and flexible in order to handle the information properly.

15. **Defensive and on guard**, making sure her rights are not violated and that she is vigilant.

16. The King of Swords reversed in her environment tells us that there is a prejudiced man over 35 attempting to influence her on this matter. His viewpoint is inaccurate and severely one-sided. **She should not take his advice**. There is a decision of some sort being cast negatively against her.

17. **Hoping for self-understanding and a new flow of feelings**. Hoping for understanding between herself and the Knight of Cups. Hopes focused on positive qualities with her new love (not past love).

18. The Six of Cups reversed indicates that our Queen of Cups may have difficulty in the future in letting go of her past. Perhaps the distressing news in the Immediate Future (Page of Swords) will cause her to revert back to dwelling on unhappy past events. The Knight of Wands influence may return because the Six of Cups reversed is an unwanted or unpleasant reunion. Her suspicion and over-emotionalism may have to be curbed in order to maintain a balanced perspective. The damage from past relationships' seen with the Knight of Wands reversed may require more weeding out in the future.

    This future card is interesting because it deals with an attitude problem; living in the past and refusing to let go. An outlook is something the Seeker can alter; therefore, in this reading the Seeker may be able to prevent the future unhappiness by **changing her attitude and not allowing past people or circumstances to dominate her**.

    When we look to the Possible Future card to confirm our interpretation, we find encouragement. The Ten of Swords reversed indicates a negative situation beginning to get better. The Seeker may change her opinion and call upon higher forces to help her. Again the concept of an outlook change is indicated. The Possible Future card suggests that hope is not completely lost, confirming our theory that the Six of Cups reversed can be altered.

    Your advice to the Seeker would be to; (1) expect some disturbing news (Page of Swords in the Immediate Future); (2) recognize that she is the Queen of Cups, which means she is subject to overemotionalism and impracticality when dealing with the affairs of her heart; (3) recognize she did indeed have a rough emotional time in her past, indicated by the Knight of Wands reversed; (4) know the Knight of Cups in her life at present is not the same type of person as the

Knight of Wands reversed in her past. Warn her that she could ruin her own future with this young man by overreacting to the forthcoming upsetting news. Suggest she apply the qualities suggested in the Page of Swords of talking and remaining flexible. Disregarding adaptability would lead to the Six of Cups reversed where she equates her past heartache with her present young Knight and refuses to see the difference between the two men.

Without changing, letting go of the past and living for today she may create the exact future for herself of which she is afraid.

The future is in her own hands. Advise her against dwelling in her past and domination from negative males, i.e., the King of Swords reversed and the Knight of Wands reversed. Warn her of her tendency to do so and point out that she can make or break her situation. Suggest she be her own best friend, as she has recently vowed.

THE MAJOR ARCANA

Lay the Major Arcana out in front of you. Choose two cards, one a favorite and one you dislike. Compare these with your first choices in Lesson 2. Now look up these two trumps' meanings.

The presence of eight or more Major Arcana cards in a reading indicates that forces of destiny or of serious psychological and spiritual import are influencing the Seeker in regard to the question.

If the reading contains a grouping of Major Arcana in the Past sections (card Placements 3 and 4) then a major crisis has occurred in the Seeker's life concerning the situation. If the cards are upright, a significant lesson concerning the Self has been learned. Reversed cards, with the exception of The Devil and The Moon, generally indicate that the Seeker has refused to deal with the self-awareness or reality that the matter has brought to their attention.

If the Major Arcana have grouped in the Present placements of the reading (Placements 1, 2, 7, 8 and 9), the Seeker is experiencing the main intensity and psychological transformations in the present. Again, reversed Majors indicate difficulties in coping with awareness about the Self and upright Majors suggest an easier integration of new awareness.

When a Major Arcana cluster appears in the Future positions (Placements 5, 6 and 10) the spiritual and psychological lessons are yet to come. Advise the Seeker that the Future cards suggest great possibilities for change and self-help if he or she is prepared to flow with the opportunities that destiny will be presenting. The future is still in the Seeker's hands. It is up to him or her to open up to the potentials, believe in personal talents and choose to make the most of the forthcoming, fortuitous situation. The Moon and The

Devil cards upright are the exceptions to this rule; in these cases the Seeker is choosing to allow selfishness (The Devil) or deception, (The Moon) to continue to rule the future circumstances.

The Major Arcana: 0-VII

THE FOOL

The Fool — Symbolism

The Fool's symbolism is a veritable treasure chest of occult imagery, but if you are unaware of this symbolism's correct interpretation, you can be led on a merry chase. Of course, the hidden representations in this first and very significant Tarot Arcana were designed precisely with the idea of concealment in mind. The occult Tarot schools valued highly the mysterious secrets contained in the Major Arcana. In an attempt to keep their mysteries from being profaned, the schools created something called a "blind."

A "blind" was the deliberate shrouding of a Tarot card with titles or symbols that led the uninitiated, no matter what their intentions astray. The Fool card is an obvious example. The very title of the card is completely misleading, so drastically that the concept the occult teachers were attempting to hide must be very important because of the extreme length to which they resorted to create a camouflage.

Here we have the Creator and its energy, power and potentials. The Fool's youthfulness represents this force and its dynamic intensity embarking on the enterprise of life. Indeed, life's adventures are represented by the image of a youth struck with wanderlust off to discover the world. The young man with his belongings in his sack seeks initiation into life through plunging into its varied experiences. This is symbolized by the character's unconcerned attitude as he descends into the ravine of the physical world.

Did you know that The Fool card actually symbolizes the Force or the Creative Power that guides the Universe? The Fool card is actually the God card in the Tarot. In this aspect it is Spirit seeking to know itself by choosing to manifest on the earthly plane and reach perfection. No wonder The Fool's potentials are so vast; they are the powers of Creation!

A variety of animals accompany The Fool on his journey into the world of matter. Many versions depict a cat either wild or tame at his heels. In some Tarot editions we find a crocodile at The Fool's feet. The crocodile is a creature whose stomach touches the ground, signifying not only the animal or sense world but the actual Earth itself, where The Fool's experiences are about to commence.

The Rider-Waite deck has a white dog as The Fool's companion, symbolizing two separate concepts. First, the dog indicates the animal or sense abilities that we use to guide us in the mundane world. Second, the dog also suggests the conscious mind that we use to analyze and define the outside universe. The theme is that of master and his faithful charge. But who really is the master, if the little dog symbolizing the conscious mind and five senses is only the friendly guide? The Fool must represent a concept vaster than these: It is the Creative God Force, much greater and larger than what we mortals usually allow to direct and motivate our life.

Traditionally, The Fool card has a white sun and yellow sky. The yellow sky indicates illumination or light. The white sun is not the one in our heavens; it is a special, spiritually pure force of white light known as "the Ancient of Days, Unity, Bliss and Oneness," translated as God, our Spiritual Source.

In many books on Tarot, The Fool is featured as a foolish, stupid action with insanity sometimes mentioned. There are three possible explanations for this interpretation. The author(s) or interpreter(s) might be atheists who feel that the Supreme Power attributed to this card is a foolish belief. Or, the author(s) could be ignorant of the true meaning of this trump and rely on the obvious interpretation of its title. The third answer is that the authors know full well what The Fool trump really means, but have prevented the disclosure of the true meaning because of an oath of loyalty to an arcane school.

No such oath is present in this author's circumstances. The introductory interpretations are honest and authentic.

The Fool — Imagery

He is Tom Sawyer and Huck Finn ambling along the Mississippi River carrying their belongings in makeshift satchels. They are out to find high adventure and learn life's lessons firsthand.

He is the prodigal son in pursuit of the phenomenon of living.

He is the innocent Parsifal seeking redemption while experiencing all the positives and negatives that the world has to offer.

He is the wandering prince and minstrel, for such persons were the laughingstock of the community because their ways differed from those of ordinary men.

The Fool is that very special quality in all of us that stirs at the thought of adventure and responds to the suggestion of a new challenge. His youthfulness symbolizes that spark of inspirational potential every person has within, waiting to be awakened and kindled by opportunity's call.

The Fool — Interpretation

Upright — Major decision and favorable opportunity.

Here we find a life-style choice or equally important option presented to the Seeker. The decision is a significant one and will bring about a change of life for the Seeker if he chooses to take on this challenge. Opportunity is the key word. The Seeker could have a chance to live in a new environment or different mode of life. Favorable circumstances may be forthcoming concerning the "possibility of a lifetime" associated with a matter that the Seeker holds dear. The Fool card denotes turning over a new leaf, starting over, a fresh start, new beginning, wiping the slate clean. The card when upright suggests that the opportunity is a good or positive one and that taking a chance may prove to be beneficial. Advise the Seeker to follow her heart's desire and to be guided by the needs of her soul.

Reversed — Foolish decision and selfish action.

When The Fool falls reversed, the Seeker may be making a poor choice. Others may dominate his thinking, or his anxieties may motivate him to choose an inappropriate course of action.

Advise the Seeker to examine his unconscious when confronting the new option or potential. Does he or she really want to be influenced by fears or someone else's dominance? Guide the Seeker toward reevaluating priorities and rediscovering what he truly desires in life. Because an opportunity of special significance may be in the offing, the Seeker should not bypass this chance.

Foolish, selfish actions are also indicated by this card reversed. Often the Seeker is participating in something where he knows he should not be involved. Regardless of the consequences, he naively continues, only to find himself embarrassed and degraded when his thoughtless deeds finally catch up with him.

THE MAGICIAN

THE MAGICIAN.

The Magician — Symbolism

The Magician is the embodiment of the belief in the strength of the mind and the power of positive thinking. He is numbered I (1), indicating that this idea is the most important thought of the Major Arcana trumps. His concept is the "I **Am** Principle" of "I am that which I think I am." He symbolizes the vitality of the conscious mind which is the key to all creativity and success. Our mental self-image — in other words, how we see ourselves — is magical, for the correct application of this notion creates our personal successes and failures. All magic truly stems from our mental programming and is our own creation. The occultists skillfully designed The Magician trump to personify these potentials of our waking mentality and to suggest the key to the unlocking of its creativity.

Confidence and faith in ourselves and our talents can create conscious, mental magic that results in self-fulfilling prophecy: we become what we imagine ourselves to be. To achieve this we must remember that our conscious minds can link with the all-potent force of the Superconscious Mind through which we tap the unlimited potential suggested in The Fool trump. The Magician, being an intelligent soul, does recall his link with the Creative Supernal (indicated by the Infinity symbol floating above his head) and is aware of the source of Infinite Potential waiting for his focus of attention.

His double-pointed wand indicates the direction of above as well as below. This suggests an individual's directing skills and ability downward into manifestation while remaining completely aware that the creative power tapped stems from a source higher than the individual's own limited intelligence.

A serious atmosphere pervades the card. We still find a youth, but his attitude has matured from the happy-go-lucky philosophy encountered in The Fool. He wears the white garment of an initiate to indicate that his intentions are sincere, while the red robe indicates that he is desirous of ambitious achievements in the world, for red is the color of passion or desire.

On his workbench we find the implements that The Fool once carried in his knapsack. The Wand denotes our will and desires; the

Cup suggests our lovingness and sensitivity; the Sword represents our thoughts and deeds; and the Pentacle symbolizes our physical body and its material requirements for survival. These implements in turn symbolize the four parts of The Magician himself, and suggest that it is the fourfold aspect of our own personality that will be worked on.

The Magician —Imagery

The Magician represents the student buckling down to conquer an assignment; the craftsperson applying discipline to achieve mastery; the professional competently accomplishing career goals.

He is the artist possessing not only the creative ability to conceive an original idea but also the coordinating ability and practical skills to carry the idea through to fruition.

Through The Fool's wanderings, life has been explored and the personal key to its fulfillment has been discovered. The time has now come to affirm one's choice by directing concentrated effort toward the attainment of mastery.

The Magician — Interpretation

Upright — The planning and directing of an ambitious creative idea or plan.

The Magician symbolizes an idea that the Seeker desires to achieve, produce or attain. The goal may be realized through dedication and concentrated effort. The circumstances are unique: The Seeker not only contemplates a plan or creative idea, but also has the talent and skills to see the idea through to completion.

This card may now be included in the selection of an Indicator card in a man's reading. The man who chooses the Magician is an ambitious person concerned with the successful accomplishment of goals. He values independence and freedom, and aims toward self-reliance and self-sufficiency.

In a woman's reading, he may indicate a man with these previously mentioned characteristics who desires to build his life around the woman Seeker. He is devoted and an active participant in their relationship.

Basically, The Magician indicates creative mental ideas or an attitude of self-confidence for both males and females.

The Seeker may be a designer, director, manager, leader or specialist who applies coordinating and guidance skills to professional or leisure pursuits.

In a legal reading he may represent a lawyer; in a medical reading he may be a doctor. Additionally he can be found in the role of teacher, adviser or counselor.

Reversed — Unrealized plans and goals.

The card's basic reversed meaning is disorganization and lack of follow-through. These traits may apply to the Seeker, the situation or a man involved with the question. The Seeker may also represent premeditatedly planning to execute an unfair, unethical action.

If The Magician indicates a man, his attributes now are less than desirable. He plots and selfishly calculates how to take advantage of situations. His promises are not kept and generally he is an untrustworthy character.

THE HIGH PRIESTESS

The High Priestess — Symbolism

A vast difference exists between The High Priestess and the two prior Major Arcana cards, The Magician and The Fool. First, we find a change in color scheme. The High Priestess is robed in blue to indicate her watery, receptive state which is unlike the outgoing, aggressive, masculine colors of red and yellow associated with The Magician.

Hers are the powers of the feminine realm, the world of the subconscious and the soul. In prior times these concepts were regarded with awe and little understanding for they were kept secret from the masses. Only an initiate could learn how to control and develop these facets and their energies. The subconscious often has water symbolism attached to it because of its flowing, reflective properties. What the water actually mirrors is the record of our personal history through the function of memory. The concept of fluidity becomes clear when we realize that the subconscious mind must be very flexible, for it first takes in everything a person has ever thought, experienced, felt, known and sensed; then it processes these experiences to create a permanent memory pattern. The water in The High Priestess card flows from her gown and quietly stands behind her as a vast sea. This sea behind The High Priestess' veil has other properties of the subconscious allocated to it. These are the psychic powers of telepathy, prophecy, clairvoyance and intuitive communication with the language of universal symbols. Through the subconscious we telepathically attune ourselves to others, receive insight into present circumstances via our symbolic dream language and are even able to predict future events. The High Priestess' number is II (2). Therefore, we see two sources of water suggesting both the personal and the universal subconscious. The two veils in the card denote two aspects of the subconscious: the psychic ability that mysteriously connects us to the past, present and future, and the subconscious capacity to reflect on and process the personal drama of our own lives.

Other dual symbols are the moons — one adorning her head in the form of a crown and the other lying at her feet. They represent change, fluctuation and cycles.

The moon's alternating schedule of full, half, new and dark indicates that The High Priestess also denotes concealed, unseen factors.

The High Priestess — Imagery

A beautiful, serene, woman quietly and intelligently pursues life in accordance with the system of her own personal beliefs.

She is the psychic peering into the past and future. She is the friend or psychologist who listens intently to us and is then able to reflect our dilemmas back to us with a comprehensive overview.

She is the historic Vestal Virgin cloistered safely behind the temple walls and kept virtuous and spiritually pure. Through her delicate attunement to the psychic world, the priests received all prophecies.

She is the soul that is veiled to us by day, but beckons us at night, filling our lives with the richness of dreams and symbolism.

She is the devout, spiritual woman, purified, devoted and dedicated. She is the subconscious powers within everyone quietly waiting to be evolved and refined.

The High Priestess — Interpretation

Upright — Factors concealed from view.

Veiled or concealed forces are affecting the question being asked. Often The High Priestess' emergence in a reading tells us that the Seeker is unsure about the question being asked. The Seeker's need is to know the future or more information concerning the question.

The High Priestess' moons symbolize changing circumstances that may be unsuspected by the Seeker. She frequently symbolizes secret, hidden forces affecting the Seeker's question regardless of the Seeker's assurance that all factors involved with the inquiry are known. The appearance of The High Priestess indicates that not all aspects of the question are known.

The High Priestess may also indicate an intuitive or psychic force within a reading. The Seeker may be inquiring about a dream or psychic feeling regarding an important matter.

This card can also represent approaching the question with high ideals and actions of a spiritual, conscientious nature. The Seeker's conduct should be governed by his or her personal, moral and ethical beliefs.

As a Final Outcome card, The High Priestess indicates the forthcoming of secret, fortuitous change. Advise the Seeker to be virtuous and encourage strict adherence to inner philosophy regarding the matter.

The High Priestess may now be included as a female Indicator card when you perform a woman's reading. A woman who selects this card for her Indicator may be described as a strongly intuitive person with a spiritual philosophy about life. This philosophy may be derived from formal religious teaching or it may have evolved naturally and independently from within this woman's own soul. Respectful of the personal rights of others, she keeps her beliefs quietly to herself, preferring to live by her actions and deeds rather than preach. The key to this woman's peace of mind and harmony lies in her adherence to her value system. She is happy when she is spiritually attuned and flowing with her intuitive awareness. Idealistic by nature, her expectations of herself and others are high and she becomes secretly disappointed when people don't live up to her standards.

In a reading The High Priestess may personify either the Seeker or a woman possessing these qualities who is involved with the query.

Reversed — Imbalance between ethics and practice leads to unhappiness. An unexpected, negative change is indicated.

The High Priestess reversed indicates that there is an imbalance between the life being lived and the personal belief system. Often this tendency manifests as compromising or sacrificing a very important personal ethic for another individual or circumstance involved in the question. The Seeker is existing within a disagreeable, compromising situation; rather than change or remedy the problem, he or she has remained dormant, perhaps developing vengeful, resentful and bitter tendencies.

THE EMPRESS

THE EMPRESS.

The Empress — Symbolism

The Empress personifies the concept of creation, growth and attraction. She finds great joy in the giving and receiving of love, indicated by the Venusian planetary rulership attributed to her and its green-like color denoting nature and growth.

Because she is female, she represents the subconscious but in a different respect than her predecessor, The High Priestess. To The Empress belong the imaginative powers of the subconscious where ideas and impressions are impregnated, take hold and finally produce our psychological picture, or programming, of what we imagine ourselves to be. This programming creates the condition of attraction or repulsion, as the case may be: love or indifference, beauty in life or sterility.

Life is a rich existence for The Empress. She has discovered the secret of giving and accepting, passion and tenderness, benefiting from the unlimited treasure of love's everflowing fountain.

The numerical concept is III (3), denoting multiplication, reproduction and formation. She is in a period of gestation. An idea or enterprise is being nourished and organized in the internal realm where it grows steadily, gaining strength for its eventual materialization or emergence into the physical world. The Empress trump is a picture of any venture in the phase of internal organization and growth prior to manifestation.

The Empress — Imagery

She is the Chinese fertility goddess, Kuan Yin, who is often depicted carrying a child

She is Venus, a Roman goddess symbolizing love, fertility and spring.

She is the aspect inherent in every person that responds to the beauty of an artistic creation, the resonance struck deep in the soul by the sound of a melodious symphony.

She personifies the instinct that answers emotionally to the miraculous birth of a child, the holding of a newborn in our arms and the witnessing of a marriage ceremony. She is the heart with which we reach out to touch life and through which life moves and stirs us.

The Empress — Interpretation

Upright — Growth, ability to give and receive love.

The basic meaning of the Empress trump is growth and development concerning any enterprise about which the Seeker may be inquiring.

Her power lies in her ability to manage, rule and attain goals through the application of affectionate and loving methods.

The Empress card signifies times of emotional and financial prosperity; the enjoyment of affections, love and family; and the ability to give and receive love.

She can be a marriage card. Marriage is one of her main attributions, as it combines the number three's concept of growth with the idea of love, resulting in an emotional relationship that becomes a nuptial union. Additionally, The Empress represents motherhood or mother.

You can now include The Empress in the selection of a female Indicator card. A woman who chooses The Empress, values the concept of fulfilling her potentials psychologically, mentally, spiritually, emotionally and economically. Such a woman aims to make something of herself and her talents, for their achievement is her key to contentment. Motherhood, marriage and family matters may be of concern to her.

Artistic, decorative, designing and creative talents are qualities also attributed to this Major Arcana card.

Reversed — No growth, blocked feelings.

The card's basic inverted meaning is stagnation. The Seeker is having difficulty in bringing about desired conditions.

The force of love that is imperative for happy functioning has been thwarted and rejected. Frustration, anger and psychological problems are the painful emotional results of these blocked feelings.

A woman who is emotionally ill may be indicated. She may feel unloved, unwanted and isolated from her own feeling nature, unable to relate to her maternal, loving and giving instincts; or she may be experiencing conception problems.

There may be rejection concerning marital ties, perhaps leading to divorce or infidelity.

Internalized anger can bring about depression and can contribute to health problems.

THE EMPEROR

THE EMPEROR.

The Emperor — Symbolism

The Emperor trump is a representation of the real or physical world made manifest. This card has the number IV (4), suggesting the foursquare, materialized universe of substance and structure. He is the concept of reality and a representation of goals and ideas achieving form.

Numerous symbols in this trump suggest that something has become real or reached actualization. This trump is ruled by the first astrological sign, Aries, indicating the springtime of the year. Spring is the season of outward growth and renewal of actions toward the external world.

The conscious mind's organizing of matter is symbolized by the return in the Tarot sequence to a male character. But now the masculine figure, The Magician, has matured, indicating that the Seeker's plan or goal is coming of age or culminating.

Red, the predominant color of The Emperor trump denotes energy, passion and action — outgoing, aggressive qualities that show the desired goal or manifested result has been intensely acted upon and successfully concluded.

The mountains in the trump's background indicate solid formation, again accenting this card's involvement with matter.

The Emperor — Imagery

He is a king, leader, governor or general. He is the Roman god Mars, the warrior who has fought in life and succeeded. He is the Egyptian god Mentu, A hawk-headed war god.

He is the part of every person who stands strong and authors his own destiny.

The Emperor — Interpretation

Upright — Plans come to pass.

The Emperor's appearance in a Tarot reading represents the manifestation or outward result of the Seeker's goals and plans.

Successful management and administration are the qualities the Seeker may be expressing in personal or professional life.

The reasoning faculty is attributed to this trump. Whereas The Empress depicts the love force and The High Priestess indicates subconscious powers, The Emperor card implies observing the outside world, analyzing it and drawing conclusions in a logical, practical manner. When you deal with this Major Arcana card in a reading, advise the Seeker to use the powers of analysis and reason to attain management effectively within the situation.

The Emperor may now be included as an Indicator card when you read for a man. The selection of this trump denotes leadership ability, emotional maturity, control, responsibility, self-reliance and independence. He may represent a self-made man or a man who desires self-government.

The Emperor evokes the father principle and suggests an authority figure, possibly a boss, official, husband or father. He personifies the father or the responsibility of fathering, including the functions of directing, controlling and decision-making. He is proud of what he has made out of his life and now is involved with the governing and management of his success. His seated position indicates dominion and rulership after efforts have been completed.

Reversed — A situation will not materialize.

The Emperor reversed indicates inaction and the collapse of plans. A venture will not manifest or mature. The Seeker lacks the ability to take charge or successfully plan a situation.

The Emperor reversed can also depict a man who is unable to deal with authority in his life. This authority may originate from a parental source, the responsibility of being a husband or father or self-confidence problems resulting in serious emotional hang-ups.

Being dependent and unrealistic causes the Seeker or a man involved with the reading to develop escapist tendencies due to an inability to cope. The character traits of The Emperor reversed are unreasonable behavior, ineffectual follow-through, disorganization and incompetence. The possibility also exists of alcoholism or other dependency problems.

THE HIEROPHANT

THE HIEROPHANT

The Hierophant — Symbolism

The Hierophant is clothed in the robes of a holy man and is seated in the reigning position of a church figurehead. He represents the standard, customary teachings and practices geared to the masses. We are asked to use faith as the kneeling monks have and accept his traditional words and laws as all we need to know.

Here again we find the Tarot scholars have constructed a mysterious blind for us to unravel. It would be very easy to accept this card at face value and neglect to look for any further interpretation. Yet The Hierophant equally indicates the teacher who dwells within, that inner inspirational feeling or instruction we are all periodically given when we calm ourselves, listen and receive.

The Hierophant's garments are the red-orange color attributed to Taurus. The combining of the sign of the bull with The Hierophant's meaning creates some thought-provoking insights. Taurus is associated with the voice and a strong, materialistic attachment to earthly possessions. The subtle inference is, do we accept as the word of God the church's orthodox, outward adornments and spoken preachings i.e., tradition designed for the unquestioning flock, or do we travel inward to commune with our indwelling, spiritual essence through our intuition and discover God within?

The word "hierophant" is interpreted as high priest; he represents spiritual authority and religious schools of thought. His monarchy is depicted by the elaborate crown and scepter he carries. Both contain three horizontal crossbars surmounted by a fourth, smaller symbol. Together they depict the four worlds or levels of creation of which he gained control in The Emperor trump.

Numerically he is number V (5), denoting change and alternation. In this card our attention turns to the inner world of spirituality, replacing the focus on reasoning and the outer world that was attributed to The Emperor.

One of the kneeling monks wears lilies to indicate that he arrived at The Hierophant's feet through his personal spiritual idealism. The other monk's robe has roses upon it to suggest his love for humanity has brought him to kneel at his teacher's throne for further guidance and instruction.

The Hierophant represents a teacher, or a person who is a Pope, guru, priest, minister or rabbi. He also personifies our spiritual teacher from within, regarded as our guide, higher self, conscience or guardian angel. The powers used in contacting this advisory source are the intuitive, subconscious powers of The High Priestess (symbolized by the silver key) that leads to the unlocking of the superconscious (indicated by the gold key). [**Note:** The colors silver and gold are difficult to detect on some card decks.]

The Hierophant — Imagery

He is the Pope of the Roman Catholic church, the minister, the rabbi, the priest, the guru, the preacher, the reverend. He is the "pontiff" or bridge between God and man. He is the soul in every person, inherently spiritual in nature. He is the intuitive part in all of us that comprehends the inner, essential value and meaning of our external experiences.

The Hierophant — Interpretation

Upright — Conservative approach regarding the question.

The Hierophant can represent the employment of a traditional, standard method or course of action. Equally it can denote intuitive guidance involved with the question. If the layout suggests job, family, medical or materialistic matters, The Hierophant then indicates conforming to the acceptable, customary method of handling the matter. The Hierophant's appearance may signify a traditional, conservative upbringing or family life.

Maritally, this card turns up for an orthodox, legal, sanctioned union, where the wife performs her classic role with the husband doing the same.

Employment may well be for a large company or organization with permanent, long-standing policies; schooling may take place in a well-established educational institution requiring strict adherence to rules and regulations. In health and medical readings The Hierophant indicates regular, standard procedures or treatments.

When a layout indicates a matter of spiritual concern, The Hierophant can be the Seeker's spiritual teacher or the intuitive inner self guiding or influencing the situation. Advise the Seeker to listen to the interior or spiritual counsel and follow the wisdom gleaned.

In many readings, the card will represent a teacher not necessarily of a spiritual nature, but simply an educator involved with the question.

Reversed — Different, unusual, original, out-of-the-ordinary way of handling a matter.

The Hierophant reversed has a meaning opposite its upright interpretation. The qualities of uniqueness, unusualness, independence and experimentation are now displayed regarding the question.

When dealing with practical matters, The Hierophant reversed suggests a new, untraditional or irregular approach. In marital readings, we find common-law ties or an unusual set of circumstances surrounding the relationship.

Medically, the Seeker may benefit from unusual, modern or experimental healing techniques.

The Seeker's employment situation may be extraordinary or unique, and schooling may have a fresh, innovative approach.

In spiritual matters, The Hierophant reversed suggests disregarding or not listening to the guidance being offered from the higher self within.

THE LOVERS

THE LOVERS.

The Lovers — Symbolism

In The Lovers trump we find three distinct characters representing three different functions of human consciousness.

The male figure in the card personifies the conscious mind with its powers of reasoning and concentration. He focuses his attention on the woman, a symbol of the subconscious mind. The female, representing the subconscious, instinctive, intuitive and emotional component, concentrates on the angel hovering in the sky. She is able to contact the archangel (Raphael), implying that her powers are the means by which we attain spiritually altered states. Raphael, the archangel associated with healing, is extending his blessings of balance, health and harmony upon the two characters. The three individuals in the card depict the triune nature within every person. We possess a conscious mental aspect involved in focusing and analyzing our world through the five senses. Also, we have a subconscious mind where memories are stored and wherein heightened sensitivity transports us into a world filled with symbolism; knowledge of the past, present and future; and the perception of inner, invisible realms. Raphael, the third member of this trinity of mind power, represents super or spiritual consciousness, the connection to the power and vibration of the Creative God Force within ourselves. On a personal level, Raphael indicates contact with the soul or spiritual essence through a conscious choice (represented by the male figure) to tap and utilize the female or subconscious powers of time, altered states, meditation and travel through dimensions. The nudity of the man and woman symbolizes honesty in the relationship.

The Lovers — Imagery

They are Adam and Eve in the Garden of Eden, man's classical Biblical confrontation with choice, temptation and correct decision-making.

The Lovers represent a marriage between two individuals in the sight of God.

Metaphysically, The Lovers can be viewed as the commencement of the mysterious alchemical marriage, a bonding between two parts of one's self or between two people, that will be fully consummated in the Temperance trump. The angel is the Archangel Raphael, healing, blending, harmonizing and balancing our mind and emotions, our lesser and greater selves.

The combining of the Anima and Animus.

The Lovers — Interpretation

Upright — Correct selection.

A decision is offered to the Seeker. To ensure a correct selection, the Seeker must know who he or she is and what is truly needed and desired for personal fulfillment.

This trump is a picture of an honest, balanced relationship, often a marriage or partnership.

The Lovers is an excellent health card because of the attribution of the archangel Raphael's healing force.

Because the card is attributed to Gemini, we have reference to the intellect or mind. Numerically the card's number is the balance and harmony of VI (6). When we combine the two concepts of mind and balance, we find mental or psychological wholeness with a harmonious integration of the conscious, subconscious and spiritual natures. On a more practical level, we have the happiness that the blending of the emotional and intellectual aspects within the self can bring.

Reversed — Incorrect decision, imbalance.

The individual is out of touch with an aspect of themselves. Perhaps they are all intellect with no feeling, or vice versa. This imbalance leads to incorrect decision-making because the Seeker is unable to discern his or her true needs.

Unwelcome suggestions or interruptions may also be present, indicating disruption from others in the planning or decision-making process. Meddling by parents, in-laws, children or others may create friction within an alliance. Inability to communicate honestly may result in a rocky romance, marriage or partnership.

Poor health can be a problem; problems can exist within the healing process.

THE CHARIOT

The Chariot — Symbolism

A fair-haired man stands strong and triumphant in The Chariot card of the Major Arcana. This is our initial encounter with a blond male, representing that the conscious mentality has combined with the subconscious powers, thereby achieving union with the superconscious. As the manifestation of the formula expressed in The Lovers card, he holds new control and balance over the outer realms of the senses, represented by the sphinxes in some versions and horses in others.

Having balanced his emotional and mental qualities, the charioteer is able to control his sensitive moods, remaining unaffected by their negative and positive fluctuations. This important control-through-balance symbolism is usually suggested in two ways: one animal is black for negativity, the other white for positivity; and one of the crescent moons on his shoulders appears as a smiling face while the other wears a frown. The charioteer is placed in the vehicle's center to indicate that he is balancing or harmonizing the opposing forces.

Great power was bestowed on the charioteer when he went through his initiation in The Lovers. The Chariot card is indeed triumph through balance, for the initiate could have easily decided to make personal, selfish use of the powers portrayed in The Lovers, getting caught up in the egotism, materialism and glamor that are indicated by the card's city background. These seductive ensnare-ments have been walled up and left behind. The spiritual portion of the inner self has disregarded the temptations, remaining stead-fast to the unfolding of the inner nature.

Cancer, the emotional sign of the soul in astrology, is attributed to this trump. In The Chariot we find the initiate's inner self taking charge and controlling the direction that the Seeker now aspires. He has discovered his "vehicle."

Seven, VII (7), is the number of victory and the unfolding of the soul. A major accomplishment in life's lessons has been achieved. The Seeker is winning in life through the balanced application of his own powers and resources and by faithful adherence to his soul's will.

The charioteer's overhead canopy filled with nightstars is sup-ported by four beams that enclose and reinforce the structure. The Chariot itself is a cube signifying an association with The Emperor trump. The structure of The Chariot signifies that we are experienc-ing mastery in the plane of reality and in our physical bodies.

The Chariot — Imagery

He is the god Shiva in his chariot drawn by five horses, each repre-senting one of the senses. He maintains complete control over his charges, reminding us of our power to rule and overcome the dic-tates of the sense kingdom.

He is Apollo, the sun god, riding across the sky in his chariot of rulership. He is Ezekiel's chariot of fire carrying mankind to the God Force.

He is the part within all people who recognize their personal power and divinity to control themselves and consequently their lives.

The Chariot — Interpretation

Upright — Mastery, winning through mind over matter, controlling the emotional and desire natures.

The combining of self-control, equilibrium and discipline has resulted in the victorious overcoming of problems and difficulties.

The emotional nature is now harmonized with reason and the intellect, making the Seeker's life more stable and less affected by sensitive moods or circumstances. The concept of "centering" is sug-gested, for the charioteer is centered in the middle of his vehicle.

How does one go about "centering"? Stop to think about what you're feeling, question the sensitivity of your thoughts, ask "Is the exterior person I present really me, or am I a different entity inside?" The sphinxes or horses are being directed through the use of some invisible control, for no reins are suggested in the picture. This occult source is mental power and correct judgment combined with love, sensitivity and mercy towards others.

The Chariot is the controlled habit card and illustrates successful dominion over negative mental attitudes, emotional oversensitivity, anger, depression or physical-psychological dependencies on food, drink, drugs, and so on.

The card's main theme suggests overcoming and mastering difficulties, then proceeds to suggest how this achievement can be attained.

Finding one's "vehicle" or particular mode of self-expression is also suggested.

Reversed — Loss of self-control, defeat.

In The Chariot card reversed our minds have gone out of control and our emotions have fallen out of balance. The Seeker has lost sight of goals and has fallen off-track. When the reading deals with habits or dependencies, The Chariot reversed indicates going off the wagon, reverting back to negative emotional habits, drugs, smoking or overindulgence in food. Poor mental and emotional programming dominate the Seeker, creating careless, reckless and self-destructive conditions.

Suggest to the Seeker that more discipline may be required or that a serious look at such self-destructive behavior may be in order.

The Chariot reversed is a failure or defeat card, possibly through loss of self-control or lack of persistence.

Review of the Major Arcana: 0-VII

COMPLETION

1. _____ is the basic function of The Emperor. He is the leading part of our personality that we use to look outward into the physical world.

2. _____, the force of harmony and attraction, is The Empress' main power.

3. The High Priestess is the image of mysteries and powers attainable through the _____ mind.

4. The Fool is the _____ or God aspect of our consciousness.

5. The intuitive, inner guardian or teacher is pictured in the _____ card.

6. The Magician is perfecting and balancing the four parts of his _____.

7. The _____ stands up in The Chariot card and proceeds to direct the course that the chariot and charioteer will now follow.

8. a. The Archangel _____ in The Lovers trump symbolizes the

   b. _____ force of God.

MATCHING

Place the trumps numbered 0-VII in front of you and correctly match each card with its meaning:

Upright Meanings

____ 1. The Fool

____ 2. The Magician

____ 3. The High Priestess

____ 4. The Empress

____ 5. The Emperor

____ 6. The Hierophant

____ 7. The Lovers

____ 8. The Chariot

a. Hidden forces

b. Materialization

c. Vast opportunity

d. Conforming or intuition

e. Decision-making

f. Creative mentality

g. Balanced victory

h. Growth and love

Reversed Meanings

____ 1. The Fool
____ 2. The Magician
____ 3. The High Priestess
____ 4. The Empress
____ 5. The Emperor
____ 6. The Hierophant
____ 7. The Lovers
____ 8. The Chariot

a. Interference with decision-making
b. Originality or not listening to inner guidance
c. No growth; problems in loving
d. Misused, misdirected power
e. Loss of emotional balance
f. Falling out of alignment with personal spiritual beliefs
g. No manifestation
h. Careless actions

Connect the card with the Character

____ 1. The Fool
____ 2. The Magician
____ 3. The High Priestess
____ 4. The Empress
____ 5. The Emperor
____ 6. The Hierophant
____ 7. The Lovers
____ 8. The Chariot

a. The teacher
b. The warrior
c. The mother
d. The devoted male
e. The spiritually dedicated female
f. The spiritual self
g. The father
h. The psychologically balanced individual

TRUE OR FALSE

Upright Meanings

____ 1. The Emperor trump indicates physical form and structure.

____ 2. The Empress card suggests the use of mind over matter.

____ 3. The Lovers signifies the three types of consciousness of humankind.

____ 4. The Hierophant suggests vast potentials and opportunities.

____ 5. The Chariot denotes hidden, secret matters.

____ 6. The High Priestess is a picture of the powers of the subconscious mind.

_____ 7. The Magician is a representation of the conscious mind.

_____ 8. The Fool personifies our emotional, loving nature.

Reversed Meanings

_____ 1. The Lovers reversed indicates psychological imbalance.

_____ 2. The Hierophant reversed suggests using mind over matter.

_____ 3. The Empress reversed can depict an angry, frustrated person.

_____ 4. The High Priestess reversed indicates that a situation will not manifest or mature.

_____ 5. The Chariot reversed is emotional imbalance bringing self-indulgent tendencies.

_____ 6. The Magician reversed shows that a person may break promises or be unable to "follow through".

_____ 7. The Fool reversed indicates one who refuses to listen to inner intuitive guidance.

_____ 8. The Emperor reversed can personify an immature, unreasonable person.

Answers to Review of the Major Arcana: 0-VII

COMPLETION
1. Reason
2. Love
3. subconscious
4. Superconscious
5. Hierophant
6. personality
7. soul
8. a. Raphael
   b. healing

MATCHING
Upright Meanings
1. **c**   2. **f**   3. **a**   4. **h**   5. **b**   6. **d**   7. **e**   8. **g**

Reversed Meanings
1. **h**   2. **d**   3. **f**   4. **c**   5. **g**   6. **b**   7. **a**   8. **e**

Connect the card with the Character
1. **f**   2. **d**   3. **e**   4. **c**   5. **g**   6. **a**   7. **h**   8. **b**

TRUE OR FALSE
Upright Meanings
1. True.
2. False. The Chariot uses mind over matter.
3. True. The conscious represented by the male, the subconscious by the woman and the God or Superconscious personified by the spiritual agent Raphael.
4. False. The Fool card is vast opportunities.
5. False. The High Priestess is the trump equated with guarding secrets.
6. True.
7. True.
8. False. Our emotional, loving nature is The Empress trump.

Reversed Meanings

1. True.
2. False. The Hierophant reversed is a card of nonconformity or refusal to listen to inner guidance.
3. True.
4. False. A situation not achieving maturity is The Emperor reversed.
5. True.
6. True.
7. False. The Hierophant refuses to heed inner revelations. The Fool reversed makes selfish, faulty choices.
8. True.

Assignment

A reading for a young woman using Major Arcana 0-VII.

Lay out the following reading:

THE INDICATOR
Indicator card — High Priestess

THE CUT
1. Queen of Wands in the Past tells us the Seeker experienced
   _____
   _____

2. Presently she is undergoing the circumstances of the Seven of Pentacles Explain. _____
   _____

3. The Future presents the forces of The Magician. Explain.
   _____
   _____
   _____

THE READING WITH OBSERVATIONS
Placement 1   Present Influence — Four of Cups
Placement 2   Helps and Obstacles — Eight of Swords
Placement 3   Past, Motivation — The Empress reversed
Placement 4   Recent Past — The Hierophant
Placement 5   Possible Outcome — The Lovers reversed
Placement 6   Immediate Future — Eight of Wands
Placement 7   Seeker's Attitude — The Emperor reversed
Placement 8   Others' Viewpoint — The Chariot
Placement 9   Hopes and Fears — Seven of Cups reversed
Placement 10   Final Outcome — The Fool

When numerous Major Arcana cards appear in a layout, the Reader may be overwhelmed by their power. True, critical life forces are at work in such a reading. Being patient and making use of the basic interpretations for these trumps will make your reading successful. In this forecast there are six Major Arcana cards, not including The High Priestess as Indicator and The Magician in the Future cut placement. These numerous Major Arcana trumps indicate that powerful and significant spiritual and psychological forces are influencing the question.

The High Priestess chosen as the Indicator card reveals that this woman possesses the attributes of spirituality, purity, psychic attunement and strong philosophical beliefs. Selecting The High Priestess denotes that she is inquiring about the unknown, unrevealed future. Her question is of major consequence, as revealed by the strong Major Arcana; her specific inquiry concerns her career.

The ten-card layout including the Indicator adds up to the number 9, characterizing the reading as a combination of achievement and confidence toward attaining the fulfillment of a cycle.

1. The Four of Cups at present suggests that_____
   _____
   _____

2. The Eight of Swords is her hindrance. Explain.
   _____
   _____

3. She experienced The Empress reversed in her Past. Elaborate. _____
   _____
   _____

4. In her Recent situation, The Hierophant card reveals:
   _____
   _____

5. Her Possible Future card reveals what she feels her future may hold. Define._____
   _____
   _____

6. What will be happening quite soon?_____
   _____
   _____

7. Her Attitude is revealed as _____
   _____
   _____

8. Others view her as _____
   _____
   _____

9. Her Hopes are revealed by the Seven of Cups reversed. Explain. _____
   _____
   _____

10. Her Final Outcome is The Fool. What does her future hold?
    _____
    _____

Answers to Assignment

A reading for a young woman using the Major Arcana 0-VII.

THE CUT

1. The Queen of Wands in the Past tells us that she met life head-on using the positive assets of her personality. Courage and friendliness have helped her to achieve goals; honesty has dictated her actions. This woman may have been in a people-related profession where she may have performed as a leader.
2. Presently she is undergoing a period of re-evaluation, possibly connected with her career (Wands) and finances (Pentacles). She has seen achievement but seems painfully aware of "something missing or incomplete" that is spoiling the present circumstances.
3. The Magician in her future denotes that there will be a definite goal or plan that she will carry through to fruition. It is also possible that an ambitious young man, The Magician, may help or influence her new direction in the future.

THE READING

1. The Four of Cups indicates that at present she has been afforded the luxury of time to retreat, contemplate and reassess her life. She has withdrawn from much participation regarding emotional matters.
2. This is obviously a Hindrance or Obstacle card. The woman may be hindered by her own indecisiveness and ambivalence as well as by interference from restrictive people and situations. She may feel imprisoned by her position and present commitments.
3. Emotional and frustrated in the Past, this young woman may have experienced problems in handling love, anger, motherhood and mothering. She has allowed her creativity to be thwarted by her destructive emotionalism and may at one time have suffered from emotional illness. Because of these past troubled bouts with her emotions, she may fall victim to her own imbalanced emotional programming again.
4. The Hierophant in her Recent Past is an indicator that she has been conforming to what is expected of her regarding the question, in this case her career. Perhaps she has been

teaching or receiving instruction. She may also have been quieting herself and going within to commune with her higher self for guidance.

5. The Lovers reversed in her Possible Future informs us that she is thinking she could make the wrong choice or have her decision interfered with in the future. There could possibly be an emotional/mental imbalance and poor psychological health. (Remember her history, i.e., The Empress reversed in her Past.) She may come up against difficulties in relationships and communication. Note that this interference factor is occurring now as suggested by the Eight of Swords in Placement 2.

6. The Eight of Wands for her Immediate Future indicates that there may be some doors opening toward new career goals very soon. Also, she may find achievements with her present career, especially the culmination of an enterprise already within reach. Advise her to expect rapid forward movement in career matters. Notice how this corresponds to the Future cut card, The Magician. Additionally, she may be traveling.

7. The Emperor reversed indicates that her attitude at present may be emotional, unreasonable and immature. She may be thinking that her professional dreams will not mature. Advise her to begin thinking more reasonably and logically about herself and suggest that quite soon she may be called upon to use her leadership, to get her life in order and to express management skills, referring to the Eight of Wands and The Magician in the Cut. An illogical, unwise man may be influencing her thinking.

8. Those around her see her as The Chariot trump, an individual following her soul's direction, who also uses great discipline and willpower. They regard her as successful, particularly in balancing her personal and professional life. They view her as having won the emotional, self-destructive war in which she was so actively engaged in the past.

9. She is hoping for a satisfactory, definite direction to become clear so that she may continue to progress.

10. The Fool card denotes a vast opportunity or potential that may unfold in her future career circumstances. She will leave her ambivalence behind and plunge headlong into this new option. Advise that she proceed based on pursuing her heart's and soul's desire. Warn her that others may try to

interfere with her choice to pursue this new venture, as suggested by The Lovers reversed in the Possible Outcome placement. Advise her that the new career goal may be more expansive than she can imagine. Foresight and purposeful, long-range goals must definitely be included in her decision-making process.

THE MAJOR ARCANA: VIII-XIV

STRENGTH

Strength — Symbolism

A beautiful white-robed woman stands amidst nature, calmly stroking an obedient red lion. In our eighth, VIII (8), Major Arcana card we encounter the theme of increase in occult power. The secret energies within human nature are of a dual nature and can now be unlocked through the forces of patience and understanding.

The Strength trump illustrates the occult maxim "know thyself." The woman in the card is aware that she partakes of a spiritual source symbolized by her pure white robe and overhead Infinity symbol. She uses her powers of understanding to quiet the lion — her desire nature; no longer do her unconscious angers and phobias dominate her attitudes and behavior. What we are actually viewing is the Tarot version of psychological analysis. Through delving into the memories that comprise our behavior patterns, we get a firm grasp on the unconscious, self-destructive behavior that can tear apart our lives. Understanding has given us the power to control the unconscious instincts represented by the lion; consequently, our first and foremost step toward self-knowledge has been achieved. Stemming from this mastery, we increase our awareness into more metaphysical areas, recognizing that spiritual occult strengths await our focus of attention.

This is the Leo card of the Tarot, the zodiacal sign of love and intelligent direction of will. Patient caring that is applied in a positive, disciplined, respectful manner contributes to the Seeker's self-loving and self-nurturing behavior. The individual then realizes that divine love is also accessible. The power the woman uses to tame the lion is not her own brute strength but strength from the power of God's love.

Strength — Imagery

She is the goddess Venus employing her enchanting ways to persuade the beast within to become tame and docile.

She is the magical woman using loving strength and spiritual understanding to achieve her aims.

She is the subconscious mind controlled, disciplined and purified. She is the Hindu goddess Kumari, who personifies the spiritual, prophetic woman.

She is the part of ourselves that is understanding, forgiving and self-nurturing, treating the self with respect and love.

Strength — Interpretation

Upright — Self-understanding, patience, self-nurturing. The use of spiritual love.

The Strength trump demonstrates the application of the power of love and understanding. The Seeker may have been or will be expressing these qualities in order to handle the question successfully.

Analysis and self-understanding help put fears and complexes into a comprehensive framework, resulting in their control. The Seeker may be experiencing a period of growth through personal or professional analysis leading to healthy self-respect and self-acceptance. This card also indicates achieving aims through kindness.

Reversed — Selfishness, lack of self-love and self-understanding.

In reversed position the Strength trump can represent dangerous psychological problems. The Seeker's behavior may be based on unconscious, uncontrolled fears; angry, violent actions are a possible manifestation. This card's appearance in a reading advises the Seeker against using pushy tactics or forcing a situation because of the agitation that can result in explosive behavior.

Misunderstandings, deliberate or otherwise, fighting and hatefulness are the unhappy manifestations of a person who dislikes himself or herself and destroys relationships.

THE HERMIT

THE HERMIT.

The Hermit — Symbolism

Alone on a mountaintop stands a sagacious pilgrim, holding a staff and bearing a lamp lighted by a six-pointed star. His journey has been an individual one; he has remained steadfast in his goal of reaching spiritual enlightenment.

The Hermit's hallmark of wisdom has been attained through the bringing together and balancing all the opposing, (black-and-white) parts of his nature, creating the neutrality of grey. Founded upon this objective and impartial point of view, his thoughts turn heavenward and his progress becomes highly accelerated.

Virgo is the sign of the loner and of service to people, demonstrating how the Seeker grew to become an initiate and in what way he will use his wisdom.

That The Hermit his reached the summit of attainment is suggested by his numerical value, IX (9).

The Hermit — Imagery

He is the saint, the guru, the mystic and the sage. He is the wise one who has traveled to the mystical mountain peak of knowledge and received enlightenment.

He is the healer, the server, or counselor who educates us by his humble example of selfless giving.

He is Hermes the Teacher who introduces us to the spiritual realms through his instruction. He is Merlin the Magician, the possessor of occult secrets and truths.

He is the part within all of us that experiences God personally and becomes a beacon of light showing and guiding others on the way.

The Hermit — Interpretation

Upright — Inner guidance, wise advice from others.
In The Hermit trump, the Seeker has attained maturity and autonomous independence, wisely and confidently executing his own decisions.

Encourage the Seeker to trust to inner judgment regarding the matter and to have the certainty and courage of conviction to carry their thoughts through to fruition.

When it does not indicate the Seeker's own wisdom, The Hermit card represents advice or guidance from a reliable source. Perhaps the Seeker will be receiving counsel from a medical, business, educational or legal professional.

A spiritual or religious teacher may offer direction to the Seeker, or suggestions are derived from a mentor.

In medical readings, The Hermit indicates the careful following of doctor's orders.

Reversed — Wisdom goes unheeded.
Reversed, The Hermit trump suggests ignoring advice that in reality should be heeded. The Seeker fails to trust or accept her own judgment concerning the matter and regrets this decision later.

Advise the Seeker to listen to her inner guidance or follow the wisdom of a counselor to ensure the correct handling of the situation.

Another possibility is that an irresponsible and immature Seeker denies any accountability for her actions.

The Seeker is inexperienced, i.e. being "green" at something.

WHEEL OF FORTUNE

Wheel of Fortune — Symbolism

The Wheel of Fortune is another misleading Major Arcana card. The orb which seems to be hurtling randomly from the heavens toward us may be taken at first glance to represent a cosmic roulette wheel! Various versions of this card portray one individual ascending to the top of the wheel while another falls from it helplessly. These dramatics imply that life is one large, continuous, uncontrollable gamble and we are at luck's mercy and happenstance while fortune and fate somehow determine our destiny.

If one looks at the surface of situations, life's distribution of benefits and hardships seem to depend on the haphazard turn of the

WHEEL ᴏꜰ FORTUNE.

Wheel of Fortune. But in studying the Major Arcana, we have learned to delve deeper into a trump's meaning to discern its true nature. Our arrival at the Wheel is through The Hermit's state of consciousness. No superficial turn of luck has brought him to the spiritual plateau he has ascended; fortune did not bring him there. As reward for the hardships endured, the initiate glimpses the working of the cosmos. The mystical letters and symbols ornamenting the wheel indicate secret universal laws that the initiate, now in a purified state, can intelligently grasp for the first time.

Jupiter, the "Great Benefic" in astrology, is the planet associated with the Wheel of Fortune, blending beautifully with the card's favorable turn of events. The number X (10) denotes the end of one cycle with the beginning of a new one about to unfold.

Wheel of Fortune — Imagery

This is the Chinese mythological Wheel of Life and Death which souls climb onto and are sent back downward, returned to form.

This is the cyclic rotation of our lives traveling from heaven to earth or from beginning to end, creating a complete revolution.

This is the Great Wheel of Time, signifying the ending of a cycle of time and the dissolving of all phenomena which reemerges later in another form.

Wheel of Fortune — Interpretation

Upright — Rewards and opportunity.

A reward cycle or fortunate opportunity. Favorable circumstances befall the Seeker. This card represents a change for the better providing expansion and growth, possibly in a new direction. The Wheel of Fortune suggests an advantageous turn of events. Advise the Seeker to lay the groundwork for success.

The Wheel of Fortune may indicate a new start into a wider, more beneficial way of life. Making the most of opportunities sometimes requires taking some calculated risks. When this card appears, the probabilities for success are very auspicious.

Reversed — Delays, hindrances and recurring problems.

A previous cycle resurfaces when the Wheel of Fortune trump turns up reversed. It signals a relapse, and what the Seeker thought was a finished matter returns to be dealt with again.

The feeling is one of little progress after much work, of ramming one's head up against a brick wall.

There are complications and delays; favorable circumstances temporarily bypass the Seeker.

The Wheel of Fortune reversed can signify a repeated mistake or the inability to have enough foresight to see an opportunity when one is presented.

Timing problems, for example, being prepared for opportunities but none occur, or vice versa.

JUSTICE

JUSTICE .

Justice — Symbolism

Justice is portrayed as a clear-seeing, well-balanced woman. Her insights and judgments are impeccable for she sees with the eyes of the universe and the laws she represents are of cosmic origin. The decisions she renders are impartial and perfectly fair. The principle of cause and effect is operating faultlessly here, meting out justice according to a celestial, not terrestrial, code and time clock.

Libra, the zodiac sign allocated to the Justice trump contains the ideas of balancing and equalizing. Justice, with her scales and double-edged sword, is seated between the two pillars of Mercy and Severity, indicating that hers is the power of decision-maker and deed-weigher. Because her authority derives from higher laws, her decisions may seem unjust or out of balance when viewed from a personal, mundane point of reference. Her spiritual rulership and cosmically impartial judgments will be proved true and correct, for they are able to sustain the test of time.

Justice's number XI (11) implies the one (1) of The Magician trump equaled by the female, personified by the duplicate one (1). Woman and her subconscious power have now been brought to a level equivalent to the male and the conscious mind. The subconscious emerges strong and purified and has assumed an equal ruling position alongside the conscious intellect.

A combination of opposite colors, coordinated to blend in a harmonious fashion, repeat the theme of balanced and successful achievements through the neutralization of inimical forces.

Justice — Imagery

She is the strong, independent, liberated woman who stands equal to anyone, male or female.

She is the Law of Karma, impartially distributing just effects for just causes. She is the divine judge and decreaser, eliminating, editing and economizing to create balance in life's proliferative abundance.

She is the destructress, the manifestation of the Hindu goddess Kali. She is the victorious war goddess, powerful and strong.

She is an aspect of the Archangel Michael, who tests and tries those desirous of the spiritual path. She is the Egyptian goddess Maat, the woman of truth who weighs the hearts of the dead and judges their deeds.

She is the aspect within all of us capable of honorable actions and reciprocal results.

Justice — Interpretation

Upright — Action, balance, positive decision. Receiving what is deserved.

Action, especially geared toward balancing the life, is the major meaning of the Justice card. The Seeker may be starting to stabilize his or her life by ensuring equal time for work and play, rest and movement, self and others, heart and mind or spirituality and materialism.

Internal prodding urges the Seeker to seek growth and change, especially in relation to obtaining fairness and developing personal goals.

Receiving what one one deserves, reaping what one has sown, and fair legal outcomes are all meanings associated with the Justice card.

Justice is also an education card in general, symbolizing schooling (sometimes in an underdeveloped area of the Seeker's life).

Reversed — Unfairness, imbalance.

Justice reversed can betoken a misjudgment. Unfair, prejudiced treatment is received by the Seeker. Rights are violated and the

Seeker does not get what is deserved. If this card appears in a legal reading, advise the Seeker not to pursue matters, for the outcome of court action will likely be unfavorable.

Educational difficulties, described as any problem with schooling from a learning block to teacher-student clashes, are additional attributes of the Justice trump reversed.

Overbearing, inflexible, merciless and prejudiced are the negative descriptions of a person or situation encountered.

An imbalance between feeling and thinking, giving and taking or work and play exists in the Seeker's life. The Seeker ignores internal prodding towards action growth and change.

THE HANGED MAN

THE HANGED MAN.

The Hanged Man — Symbolism

Another of the most misleading cards of the Major Arcana is The Hanged Man. In time past he was known as "The Drowned Man." At present he is undergoing a rejuvenation as "The Suspended Man" of the Tarot.

Neptune, the planet of illusion or enlightenment, is the ruling cosmic force, offering us a key to the impasse this Tarot blind creates. To "hang" is to suspend, **give up**, surrender or sacrifice something, often exchanging the lesser thing for the greater. Mystically speaking, what is being put in reversed position is our egotistical desires and reliance on our own cleverness to see us through life's struggles. The Hanged Man's inverted position indicates that abandoning dependence on our own smartness and self-importance is contrary to the ways of the world. The character in the card seems unmoved by others' opinions of his choice of priorities which are now reversed from the common person's and directed toward spiritual unfolding, and alignment with God's knowledge. The facial expression and halo encircling the character's head reveal to us that he is not suffering. He is relieved and pleased with his choice to cease worrying and trying to outwit life and death. His life is in the Higher Force's hands; his passion and actions, symbolized by the red lower garment, are stilled; his subconscious, symbolized by the blue upper garment, is freed of its burden of memory and recall. Action, passions, desires, memories and ego-intellect, signified by the yellow shoes, are unimportant. Only The Hanged Man's spirituality directs his being.

The card's number is XII (12), combining the number one (1) of The Magician's conscious mind with the number two (2) of the female, subconscious principle. Both are relinquishing their fundamental functions and principles to make way for the total initiation into spirit. Samadhi is the yogic, meditative goal demonstrated where the subconscious and conscious mind are stilled in preparation for the grace of divine union.

The rope, a representative of our direct line and support to the cosmic, suspends The Hanged Man from a living tree, symbolic of life in the spirit.

The Hanged Man — Imagery

He is Christ on the cross, aware that his cruxifixion will bring light and salvation to mankind.

He is the guru assuming the state of Samadhi where he will "know" and attain enlightenment. He is the water god Neptune plunging into the depths of the spiritual sea.

He is the mystic living a life of complete renunciation, sacrificing all in order to reach complete union with Divinity. He is the "Slaying of the Ego" which in India is taken as a prerequisite step before Nirvana.

He is our innate spirituality discovered through the sacrifice of the ego and the surrender of our will to God's will.

The Hanged Man — Interpretation

Upright — Renunciation, sacrifice, change in priorities.

Sacrifice usually implies the painful giving up of someone or something that the individual holds dear. In some instances The Hanged Man does symbolize this difficult surrender. Sacrifice can also imply a forfeiting of one thing to attain something better. Both interpretations are applicable. If there are difficult cards involved with the reading, then the former meaning applies. If the cards are more beneficial, employ the latter meaning.

Spiritually, a sacrifice represents dedicated service, worship and making an offering to the Creator. The Seeker is advised to place the problems in the Higher Force's hands and have faith that the situation will be resolved the way it is "meant" to be.

Reversal is the other basic meaning of this card. The Seeker may encounter an alteration or rearrangement of values, priorities or belief system. The Seeker's outlook may become the opposite to an original stand. If the Seeker lives in the country and The Hanged Man appears in a moving or relocation reading, then the Seeker may soon be residing in the city. If the Seeker has a sedentary desk job and the reading suggests change of employment, The Hanged Man qualifies this by indicating a job of opposite type, perhaps an active, traveling position. The reversal may be in life-priorities where the Seeker stops considering others first and places personal needs first, or vice versa.

Being uncertain, hung up or in limbo regarding a situation can also be interpretations of The Hanged Man when it appears with negative cards.

Reversed — Materialism, pride, ego and selfishness.

Materialism, pride, ego and selfishness are "hang-ups" preventing the Seeker from seeing any viewpoint except his or her own.

Immovability and narrow-mindedness create the inability to "let go and let God."

Self-centeredness and an insistence on having things one's own way prevent improved conditions.

DEATH

DEATH.

Death — Symbolism

Infamous and frightening, the Death trump of the Tarot personifies everything "bad" about card reading. This unfortunate Arcana card taken at face value, appears ominous, threatening our well-being and psychological wholeness. By now, however, we realize that what appears on the surface of a Tarot card rarely reveals its true nature.

Because this is the Scorpio card of the deck, we must delve especially deeply behind the exterior, for Scorpio is the sign of occult mysteries and secret activities. In the horoscope wheel Scorpio does govern death and rebirth. The secret lies in the knowledge that we can detach from emotional and mental attachment to our forms (symbolized by the skeleton) and still inhabit the earth. If the trump signified physical death, the skeleton would also be in a disintegrating, passive state, which it is not. The white horse symbolizes the self of our physical desires which previously appeared as the white dog of The Fool and the red lion of Strength, in a perfectly purified condition. It is that precise condition that facilitates the "rebirth" or transformation that this trump truly heralds. The sunrise indicates a new dawn, and the river's sharp turn shows that our direction is being purposely rechanneled toward that metamorphosis, similar to death, that can occur for every person.

The number one (1) of the conscious mind has combined with the number three (3) whose concept is growth and imagination to form the number XIII (13). Our imagination has expanded to a point where we realize and envision our own transfiguration.

The black banner decorated with a white rose in full bloom, suggests that we have come to an abyss where we can choose to shed our past and eliminate our previous existence. We then assume the position of refinement prepared for the spiritual Sun and celestial waters to nurture us into replete, newborn splendor.

Death — Imagery

This is the Egyptian god Chaos, known as Nun or Nu, who represented the concept of the primordial ocean from whence all seeds of life sprouted.

He is Saturn in Grim Reaper form, carrying the sickle that will cut away all visible growth.

He is every person experiencing a new liberation and freedom through realizing the soul's immortality.

Death — Interpretation

Upright — A welcome change, new beginnings. Emotional growth and transformation.

The Death trump is an excellent card to receive in a reading, for it proclaims a positive, liberating change. A brand-new way of life begins, a different cycle commences; hopes for the morrow are fulfilled.

Moving may be indicated, either in domestic or professional locale or within the Seeker's outlook, for the past has been left behind.

Emotionally this is a superb Major Arcana card because it betokens the transformation of the feeling aspect of life. Old emotional programming ceases to trip up the Seeker, who is now free from a destructive, neurotic, overly sentimental nature. A serene, healthy lovingness assumes the past unhappy place.

Reversed — Inactivity.

A standstill situation, a deadlock or dormant position brings the Seeker to an impermanent impasse. This, too, shall pass; movement regarding the circumstance is still ahead.

TEMPERANCE

Temperance — Symbolism

The Temperance trump provides us with the second Archangel of the Tarot series, Michael. "He who is as God" or "God-like" are the phrases associated with him. Indeed, the Death trump's transformation would endow us precisely with the God-like qualities Michael represents, for the rest of us, our dross, has been drained away.

Sagittarius, the sign of the high-aiming archer with his bow and arrow, is the designated astrological ruler of Temperance. This constellation of the zodiac pertains to high ideals of religious and spiritual visions. These philosophical concepts are no longer abstract unknowns to the initiate, for he has attained victory over another phase of balance, the moderation and adaptation between the physical world and life in the spirit. This highly skilled balancing is accomplished by the focusing and channeling represented by the number (1) combined with the inner vision or awareness of spirit lying behind all forms of matter the associative meaning of the number four (4), to form XIV (14).

The white robe of virtue and the triangle within a square, symbol of an adept, comprise Michael's garb. A crownlike sunburst rises on the horizon, while irises, the flower named after a Greek goddess who personifies rainbows, reiterate the promise of "as on Earth, so it is in Heaven."

Temperance — Imagery

Temperance is the Archangel Michael administering tests and bestowing rewards as a direct assistant to Christ.

Temperance is the Greek goddess Iris, personified by the rainbow, who was the female messenger of the gods. Temperance is Diana the huntress, aiming her bow and arrow heavenward toward spiritual attainment.

Temperance is the angelic part in every person that rises as a phoenix from the mire and is subsequently tried and tested.

Temperance — Interpretation

Upright — Stabilizing or adjusting.

Equilibrium, cooperation and adjustment are the true implications of the "tempering" behavior of this Major Arcana card. The Seeker is called upon to meet others halfway, behave agreeably in order to handle circumstances and compromise. The approach is a moderate, middle-of-the-road stance.

Timing is an important factor of this card. When upright, the indications are of correct synchronization and the blending of right circumstances, (e.g., the proper person for the job, appropriate teacher for the student, lovers well suited for each other, and so forth).

This card can also pertain to a test in the Seeker's situation. This may manifest as a trial period or trying situation, where the individual's philosophy is put to the test. A difficult dilemma may require the Seeker to put beliefs into practice. Other references to testing are simply an educational or medical exam of some sort, which the Seeker will pass when the card is upright.

Temperance is the art card and can also represent the Sagittarian flair for teaching.

Reversed — Radical, improper action.

Extremist in behavior, the Seeker finds himself way out on a limb. The inability to handle situations, a lack of compromise and excessiveness have brought the Seeker to this precarious position. An overreactive, impatient and irritable nature causes the Seeker to bungle the situation. Advise the avoidance of immoderate, drastic and unreasonable behavior. Suggest negotiation and compromise for the creation of harmony.

Tests are failed. If one's spiritual or philosophical beliefs are being tested, the inability to act in accordance with one's beliefs creates this failure.

Review of the Major Arcana: VIII-XIV

MATCHING
Place the trumps numbered VIII-XIV in front of you and correctly match each card with its meaning.

Upright Meanings

_____ 1. Strength	a. Inner wisdom
_____ 2. The Hermit	b. Reversal, sacrifice
_____ 3. Wheel of Fortune	c. Opportunity knocks
_____ 4. Justice	d. Freedom, change
_____ 5. The Hanged Man	e. Timing, managing
_____ 6. Death	f. Love, self-understanding
_____ 7. Temperance	g. Balance, education

Reversed Meanings

_____ 1. Strength	a. Setbacks, relapse
_____ 2. The Hermit	b. Poor management
_____ 3. Wheel of Fortune	c. Standstill
_____ 4. Justice	d. Selfishness, egotism
_____ 5. The Hanged Man	e. Unfairness, imbalance
_____ 6. Death	f. Self-hatred, pushiness
_____ 7. Temperance	g. Immaturity, rejection of wisdom

Connect the card with the Character

_____ 1. The divine, cosmic judge; the law	a. Strength
	b. The Hermit
_____ 2. The archangel of godlike qualities	c. Wheel of Fortune
	d. Justice
_____ 3. The orb of opportunity	e. The Hanged Man
_____ 4. The wise sage, adviser or teacher	f. Death
	g. Temperance
_____ 5. The renouncing mystic	
_____ 6. The reborn, liberated self	
_____ 7. The understanding, loved self	

TRUE OR FALSE

_____ 1. The Hermit reversed indicates lack of wisdom, immaturity and irresponsibility.

_____ 2. The Wheel of Fortune denotes delving into one's psychological programming.

_____ 3. When Death appears, the Seeker should prepare to meet his or her maker.

_____ 4. Health tests and exams in general are passed with the Temperance card.

_____ 5. Injustice and prejudiced, overly severe actions are the upright meanings attributed to Justice.

_____ 6. The Hanged Man indicates a sacrifice or surrender that should be avoided at all costs.

_____ 7. The Wheel of Fortune upright suggests endowment of opportunity; if it is reversed, the chance bypasses the Seeker.

_____ 8. The Hanged Man reversed has selfishness, narrowness and stubbornness associated with it.

_____ 9. Strength applies love, patience and unselfishness to the matter.

_____ 10. Temperance reversed indicates stagnation.

_____ 11. The Death card reversed indicates mismanagement and radical, extreme behavior.

_____ 12. The Hermit upright can suggest valuable advice from within oneself or from others.

_____ 13. Justice is an education card.

_____ 14. Strength reversed indicates emotional confusion raging within the Seeker.

Answers to Review of the Major Arcana: VIII-XIV

MATCHING

Upright Meanings
1. **f**   2. **a**   3. **c**   4. **g**   5. **b**   6. **d**   7. **e**

Reversed Meanings
1. **f**   2. **g**   3. **a**   4. **e**   5. **d**   6. **c**   7. **b**

Connect the card with the Character
1. **d**   2. **g**   3. **c**   4. **b**   5. **e**   6. **f**   7. **a**

TRUE OR FALSE

1. True.
2. False. The Strength card is the psychoanalysis trump.
3. False. The Death card doesn't indicate a demise. It symbolizes rebirth and liberation.
4. True.
5. False. These are the reversed meanings of Justice.
6. False. The sacrifice or exchange will benefit the Seeker.
7. True.
8. True.
9. True.
10. False. The Death card reversed is stagnation.
11. False. The Temperance card reversed indicates this.
12. True.
13. True.
14. True.

Assignment

A reading using the Major Arcana VIII-XIV.

THE INDICATOR
Indicator card — King of Pentacles

THE CUT
Past — Ten of Pentacles reversed
Present — Justice reversed
Future — Strength reversed

Note: It is possible to have all three cards reversed in the Cut. Handle this as you would in the layout.

1. Judging from the Indicator card, who is the King of Pentacles and what may be his uppermost concern?

   _____

   _____

   _____

2. The King of Pentacles has experienced problems in certain areas of his life. Name these areas and describe the possible problems.

   _____

   _____

   _____

3. What would you, the reader, ask upon seeing the Justice card reversed in the Seeker's Present cut?

   _____

   _____

   _____

4. The Strength card reversed suggests certain advice and warnings. How would you handle these?

   _____

   _____

   _____

THE READING

Placement 1	Present Influence — The Hanged Man reversed
Placement 2	Helps and Obstacles — The Hermit
Placement 3	Past, Motivation — Three of Wands
Placement 4	Recent Past — Five of Pentacles
Placement 5	Possible Outcome — Death
Placement 6	Immediate Future — Wheel of Fortune reversed
Placement 7	Seeker's Attitude — Ten of Swords
Placement 8	Others' Viewpoint — Four of Pentacles reversed
Placement 9	Hopes and Fears — King of Swords reversed
Placement 10	Final Outcome — Temperance

1. The card reading adds up to the number 8. What is the theme of the reading? _____

2. The Hanged Man reversed in the Present placement indicates:

_____

3. The Hermit crosses him. Explain. _____

4. How did things look in the Past? _____

5. How has the Seeker faired recently? _____

6. What does the Possible Future hold? _____

7. What is the Seeker soon to experience? _____

8. His thoughts are symbolized by the Ten of Swords. Explain.

_____

9. How do others view his dilemma? _____

10. What are his fears? _____

11. What does his Future hold? _____

Answers to Assignment

A reading using the Major Arcana VIII-XIV.

THE CUT

1. The King of Pentacles is a responsible, mature man, a hard worker and a materialist. He is practical, traditional and conservative by nature. He may be concerned about his money and finances remaining secure.
2. The King of Pentacles has experienced instability in either job and financial matters or within his family. The problems may have been of an embarrassing nature, perhaps concerning risks he should not have taken.
3. Ask the Seeker if he is presently dealing with some type of prejudice or unfairness, possibly a legal problem. Is he in the middle of a lawsuit?
4. The Strength card reversed warns the Reader that the Seeker may attempt to force or push an issue that should not be forced. Warn the Seeker to watch out for confrontations from opposing factions that could cause him to lose his temper and behave irrationally.

THE READING

1. The theme of the reading is money and power.
2. The Seeker is being selfish and immovable about an issue. A sacrifice is being demanded of him on which he refuses to budge because of financial or egotistical reasons. He is relying on his wits and cleverness, insisting he knows all the answers.
3. A wise counselor is attempting to help the Seeker. Good advice is helpful to him but the question may be, will he heed it? It would help the situation if the Seeker did listen, indicating the resolution of the present Hanged Man reversed problem!
4. In the past the Seeker experienced growth, cooperation, teamwork and good results concerning ambitions.
5. Recently he has had his beliefs crushed and has experienced financial loss.
6. Possibly he will be free of these financial difficulties, legal problems and pressures, represented by the Five of Pentacles and Justice reversed in his present cut. Perhaps he will make a new start.

7. Soon he will encounter another setback. The Wheel of Fortune reversed warns him that problems he thought settled will recur. Perhaps his legal battles will incur setbacks. He may allow opportunities for improving conditions to bypass him. He may not listen to The Hermit's advice.

8. The Ten of Swords suggests a defeatist attitude. He is of the opinion that he is ruined and that all is lost.

9. Others view him as losing control of his situation. They see him falling apart at the seams and experiencing financial setbacks.

10. His Fears revolve around his lawsuits. The King of Swords reversed personifies those fears, as well as his being frightened about a ruthless lawyer who may be involved with the case. He fears unfair accusations and a prejudiced decision.

11. His Future holds successful adaptation and meeting his opponent halfway. He may find a legal outcome more fairly balanced then he anticipated. He will be required to make some adjustments and meet others halfway. His patience and tolerance as well as his personal principles may be tested. Advise him to prepare for this test by expecting this and rising to the occasion by being honorable. Willingness to negotiate will help. He will be able to manage the outcome of this situation successfully by anticipating the use of ethical procedures and by being cooperative. The compromise will be manageable. His Possible Future, the Death card, confirms that he can see freedom from his problems. The Future cut card, Strength reversed, warns him not to push or behave selfishly and irrationally.

THE MAJOR ARCANA: XV-XXI

THE DEVIL

The Devil — Symbolism

The Devil is a horrendous creature composed of bat's wings, eagle's claws and a goat's head. The message the Tarot scholars were aiming to represent is obvious: This creature does not exist! The figure mounted on a half-drawn cube symbolizes the distortion of reality that judgment based on outward appearance can bring. This ignorance of believing only in what our five senses tell us is reinforced by the dullness of the man's and woman's eyes and their seeming unawareness of the bondage and limitation of their vision, depicted by the chains. A black background of alien darkness symbolizes the fear of the unknown and unfamiliar that we all occasionally experience. The key to handling these devilish anxieties lies in our refusal to become imprisoned by them through treating them with humor and common sense.

Capricorn, the astrological sign of The Devil trump, is known partly for materialistic and power-mongering tendencies. We find the Devil's enslavement to keeping up appearances concerned especially with material show. Mankind's consciousness has been perverted. This is represented by the inverted star on The Devil's forehead, suggesting that our thoughts are directed toward terrestrial, not celestial, matters. Capricorn is a sign that can indicate secret fear and allowing worry and concern to motivate one's thoughts and actions.

Numerically, we discover the one (1) of conscious mind incorporated with the five (5) of undesirable change and disruption, giving the number XV (15). The change of direction in The Devil card is from the spirituality and divine powers witnessed in the prior trump, Temperance, to the worship of materialism and participation in selfish power games.

The Devil — Imagery

He is Pan, the nature god who first appeared to the world with the legs, horns and beard of a he-goat. He was associated with fertility and the protection of sheep.

He is Lucifer, the angel who fell to earth because he asked God for too much power. He is Saturn, a Roman deity associated with farming and abundance. Known for growing vines and hard work in the fields, Saturn brought about a plentiful harvest.

He is the negative, demonic side of all of us, tempting us to disregard life's morals and urging us to misuse one another.

The Devil — Interpretation

Upright — Encountering personal fears.

Making errors by basing judgments and decisions on fears.

Role-playing, materialism, vanity, superficiality and outward show are symbolized. The Seeker may have a preoccupation with money and is involved with impressing others through maintaining appearances.

The Devil is a fear card. One's fears are the enemy. Fear causes enslavement to a very limiting situation. The individual is stuck in the role that must be played and is afraid of changing out of it.

Maritally, The Devil card can represent bondage to a marriage for appearance, convenience or money.

The Devil card is often a mistake trump when indicating a decision. Often the Seeker is considering a choice that will be wrong because his judgment is clouded by fears and not based on facts. Temptation exists specifically in doing something strictly for the money or to manipulate people or circumstances.

Reversed — Freedom from worries, opponents and materialism.

Fears are released. Vanity, enemies and selfish needs are overcome. The Seeker no longer allows others to keep him or her in a role that is uncomfortable.

Lessons concerning greed and possessiveness are learned.

The Seeker refuses to misuse personal power and manipulate others.

THE TOWER

THE TOWER.

The Tower — Symbolism

Lightning strikes a high, man-made tower; two individuals fall from its lofty heights. The Tower is crowned with glittering illusions; the man and woman encased themselves in a narrow structure of egotistical beliefs of superiority. The wrath of God, attributed astrologically to Mars, has struck this symbol of materialistic delusion, bringing truth, reality and enlightenment in its wake.

A creative life force, the Yods, rains down in symbolic patterns, bringing new life energy and washing away old forms.

This is the truth and enlightenment card that brings awakening and a new perspective, often at the expense of the Seeker's delusions if there is something hidden to face.

Spiritually, this trump is very welcome, for it presents the Seeker with new insight and understanding concerning an aspect of personality or philosophical programming that has kept him or her isolated and unable to fully know God.

The number one (1) of the conscious mind has experienced the influx of an awakening on a spiritual level, referring to the workings of the formula from The Lovers card, trump VI (6) forming the number XVI (16).

The black background in The Tower is similar to the previous Arcana card. In contrast to The Devil trump, however, the darkness now has been blessed with the addition of light — a symbol of divine power, enlightened consciousness and spiritual truth.

The Tower — Imagery

This is the Tower of Babel, a physical outer structure built high enough to reach heaven. God frowned upon this and ordered humankind to speak in various languages because inner spiritual growth had been confused with external, rational and materialistic ways.

This is also the Mother-Lightning goddess Tien Mu in Chinese mythology and the Pawnee Lightning God who explored and enlightened the tribe about Earth.

The Tower is the power of the Roman god, Mars, who symbolizes fertility — as does lightning. Mars also is the god of battles and "War," the alternate title of The Tower trump.

The Tower is the enlightening and awakening that occurs in every person discovering the truths of God. A fertile foundation for personal spiritual growth has now been laid.

The Tower — Interpretation

Upright — The truth surfaces — An awakening.

The Tower trump is difficult if the Seeker is not facing something. This is the truth and honesty card, which in this case comes as a shock or bolt from out of the blue to the Seeker. Selfish and manipulative tendencies will be exposed, and a situation will be seen for what it truly is.

The Tower can be a positive card if the Seeker desires fuller self-knowledge, for circumstances bring revelations about motivation and character that can be very enlightening.

If the reading concerns a health question, breakdowns through nerves or illness are indicated. More often this breakdown or change pertains to a routine or structure that involves the Seeker's employment or job environment, home, family, marriage or psychological programming or any arrangement where the format will be altered.

Reversed — Manageable crisis. Expected change.

The Tower's basic interpretation of circumstances breaking down and changing remains the same when in reversed position. The Tower reversed can suggest that the Seeker knows about the breakdown and is not completely shocked or caught off-guard. Sometimes the crisis is less severe.

Truth brings positive change, for the Seeker is no longer imprisoned by his own or someone else's selfishness or ignorance.

THE STAR

The Star — Symbolism

A female figure, nude to personify honesty and purity, calmly dips a clay jug into a pool of water while simultaneously pouring liquid from another clay jug onto the land. She is taking from one realm and distributing to another, much like her astrological counterpart, Aquarius the Water-Bearer. The scene actually depicts the meditation process attributed to The Star card, where the individual subconscious, personified by the woman, dips into the reservoir of the universal subconscious, and applies those revelations to the conscious earthly realm of everyday life.

The center star indicates the soul of the spiritual self and its enlightenment or unfolding as the meditation process continues. The surrounding stars symbolize the personal astral energy centers called chakras that are affected by meditation. The bird, symbolizing the conscious mind, sits on the tree, quietly observing the cosmos unfolding.

The card's number is XVII (17), this time combining the self-conscious number one (1) with the perfect mental control of The Chariot trump, number VII (7), to bring about the soul's unfurling and freedom to flow.

The Star — Imagery

She is the greek goddess Urania, the Muse of Astronomy, who carried the compass and an orb of the universe.

She is Isis in her cosmic manifestation as the subconscious dipping into the pool of the universal mind and soul. She is Aphrodite, Urania the stellar goddess of aesthetic, ideal and pure love.

She is the Greek goddess Astarte and the Egyptian goddess Ashtart, considered as Venus, the most beautiful planet of the cosmos. She is Nut, the Egyptian goddess of the sky, often pictured with a vase, who gave birth to the sun and whose belly represented the sky and its stars.

She is the beautiful, celestial part of all of us, unfolding as a flower with the growth of our souls through meditation.

The Star — Interpretation

Upright — Talents, desires and dreams.

The Star trump symbolizes the Seeker's dreams and aspirations. Often it denotes the pursuit of natural talents with confidence, enthusiasm and dedication.

Also symbolized by The Star trump is an inspired goal which may be chosen and followed through.

Additionally, The Star card suggests positive thinking and good mental and physical health.

Meditation, where the Seeker finds new insights and revelations, is symbolized by this trump. Encourage the development of this mental exercise as means for the Seeker to find new personal talents and potentials and to reach inspired, creative goals.

Reversed — Talents and hopes defeated.

The Star forfeits all of its optimism when reversed.

Poor health-emotional, mental and physical — may be indicated. This negativity may result from the Seeker's poor self-image. One may think so poorly of himself that creative ideas and potentials are sabotaged because the Seeker deems them invalid or unimportant. Depression and insecurity incapacitate the Seeker so that individual assets and talents go unseen. A lack of inspiration and sense of hopelessness dashes aspirations. Encourage the individual to be aware of this damaging negativity and to seek counseling or begin a program of self-help. Often when I see this card in a client's future, I inquire what he does to relieve depression and negativity. I suggest that a difficult period may emerge and to be prepared to employ that personal remedy to the negative situation.

THE MOON

The Moon — Symbolism

The Moon reigns supreme in a night-time sky; her color is golden, for she reflects the Sun.

Hers is the world of dream and subconscious memory, where our evolutionary racial history is stored. The Moon card is actually a picture of evolution. In the foreground our emergence from the sea is depicted by an ancient crustacean in some Tarot versions and an Egyptian scarab carrying its egg in others. Next, we have the mineral world symbolized by the rocks and the vegetable world represented by the plants and grass. The animal kingdom is depicted

THE MOON.

both in its wild, untamed phase by the baying wolf and in its tame, modified state by the dog. Humankind is symbolized by these two creatures also, for as we become less barbaric and more refined, we continue up the golden central path, passing beyond the two outposts of the conscious and subconscious mind into the unknown realm of the psychic, astral world. The Moon card has peril and danger attributed to it, because when we go into the psychic, astral realms we enter an unknown, potentially deceptive realm of illusions, misinterpretation, self-deception and unrealistic living. The idea is to remain steadfast on the golden, spiritual path and use the astral, psychic worlds as a ladder to the mountain top of godly attainment where The Hermit awaits us.

Surprisingly, The Moon card is ruled astrologically not by Cancer but by Pisces. Pisces is the naturally intuitive sign of the zodiac. People who live out the negative aspects of Pisces often fall prey to deception and self-delusion, preferring a dream-fantasy world over the reality and mental clarity needed to deal effectively with everyday life.

The number one (1) of conscious mental power combines with the understanding and control of our subconscious programming and power, the number eight (8) forming XVIII (18). A path opens that offers spiritual attainment through adapting the two modes of thinking to a higher purpose.

The Moon — Imagery

This trump's secret unseen god is Anubis, an Egyptian deity associated with guidance into the "other world." Anubis possesses the countenance of a jackal or the head of a dog.

All the Moon goddesses with their various roles of illusion, enticement and enchantment are affiliated.

The Moon is the Piscean Edgar Cayce, a modern mystic who had the ability to enter into a powerful trance state. He communicated with the Akashic Records to bring answers concerning life and medicine to mankind.

The Moon is the subconscious dream, psychic and astral states within every person.

The Moon — Interpretation

Upright — The Moon card represents dishonesty from within oneself or from others. The Seeker may be victimized by someone's pulling the wool over her eyes, may be lying to herself, or may be behaving deceitfully in general.

The Moon, because it represents fluctuation, can personify unexpected changes and sudden new information that causes disruption when exposed. Discovering these hidden facts may be unpleasant, and the Seeker may become confused, disillusioned and hurt. Caution and carefulness are advised, because no matter what the Seeker claims to know about the matter, some important factors still remain unrevealed.

The Moon may also be interpreted as the psychic trump, indicating intuitive sensing and the astral, clairvoyant world. Sleeping and dreaming are also symbolized.

If the Seeker's cards do not indicate the distressing nature of the Moon's first meaning, then the latter psychic interpretation may be applicable. The Seeker may feel psychic about the matter in question, or a dream or vision may be the topic. In this case, The Moon simply signifies experiencing an altered, psychic state.

Reversed — Dishonesty ends. The Moon trump is more favorable when in the reversed position. The idea of dishonesty is removed, and the unexpected change of upright position becomes little more than an expected, positive change or alteration requiring little adjustment.

Confusion and self-deception diminish; honest love and caring surface.

This is an excellent card of creativity for anyone who desires to organize a plan or dream, because it denotes putting together the pieces of a creative enterprise and making it work.

Reversed, The Moon can still symbolize psychic activity.

THE SUN

The Sun — Symbolism

In addition to its own straight, angular light beam, The Sun radiates the wavy, intuitive lines shown on the ground and path of The Moon card. The conscious mind represented by the angular lines and the subconscious, symbolized by the wavy, have been freshly integrated into a new level of personal wholeness and oneness represented

THE SUN .

by the face in the Sun. In other words, a personal rebirth or transformation has occurred. The individual has successfully combined and balanced the divergent aspects of the self. The spiritual self has been born, as the child in the card suggests. We are now newborns in the spiritual realm. We are safe, protected, trusting, open and free. The white horse indicates the taming and purification of the basic sensate self, for the child now controls this aspect effortlessly. The victory flag and wreath are again evident, pointing to our new accomplishment of rebirth. The sunflowers all turn to the child for their source of energy. Their full development indicates mastery of skills, independence and self-reliance.

The Sun itself rules this Tarot card. Birth and rebirth are intimated, for when the planetary Sun returns to the place in the heavens where it appeared when we were born, we celebrate that return as our birthday.

The number one (1) of self-consciousness is now integrated with the number nine (9) of attainment and fulfillment, forming XIX (19); therefore, achievement on the intellectual as well as the wisdom level of mentality is indicated.

The Sun — Imagery

He is Ra, the Egyptian Sun God who created all subsequent Egyptian gods and goddesses. He is Apollo, the Greek god of sunlight, and Helios, the personification of the actual Sun itself.

The Sun has a concealed aspect of Christ, for it represents the internal spiritual rebirth attainable by every person.

The Sun — Interpretation

Upright — Rebirth, personal transformation.

The Sun card brings happiness, accomplishments and self-fulfillment.

Mastery is also indicated in educational, technical, career and artistic matters.

The Sun can be a marriage card when a reading deals with family, love or romance.

Good health and the successful overcoming of illness can be indicated.

The ideas of leadership and authority are symbolized with the Seeker in the role of chief or head of a situation.

Rebirth, where the individual overcomes problems and becomes a new person filled with positiveness, health and successful self-expression, is one of this trump's main meanings. This rebirth may manifest itself by a change in wardrobe, hairstyle, appearance or attitude that physically projects the newborn, independent self. Self-reliance, self-disclosure, trust and openness are additional manifestations of the growth characterized by The Sun card.

Protected and safe circumstances prevail.

Reversed — Defeat and emptiness.

The Sun card reversed indicates emptiness, lack of fulfillment and the inability to imagine a way out of these depressive conditions.

Failures can prevent the Seeker from trying to help himself. Negative, fearful and narrow thinking can prevent the Seeker from trying to bring about change.

A marriage or relationship may be unsuccessful.

JUDGEMENT

Judgement — Symbolism

The Judgement trump presents us with our third Archangel of the Tarot, Gabriel, whose name signifies "Strength of God."

We could interpret this scene as the Last Judgement with the dead rising from their graves, but how would this apply on a personal level? Surely not as death and resurrection, for we do not read death in Tarot. Again the occultists who designed the Tarot challenge us to search deeper for the trump's true meaning.

Gabriel, resplendent with banner and horn, awakens the grey souls from their earthly limitations or encasement in form. They arise, summoned by the sound of a spiritual, vibratory call and experience a transformation into the consciousness of spiritual unity and wholeness.

A great ocean, which first appeared behind The High Priestess, symbolizes the universal subconscious. About to be absorbed into this ocean are the individual subconscious, represented by the female; the individual conscious mind or the male; and the newborn, the spiritual self.

The numerical association with Judgement is XX (20). This is your first encounter with two (2) as the leading digit. The subconscious mind and its vast ocean-like potential have now attained a superior position, indicating a transformation from the usual dominance of the conscious mind. Both the personal and the universal subconscious power first discovered in The High Priestess have now blended with the pure energy light (the spiritual God Force) of The Fool, number zero.

Pluto, the planet of psychological power and transformation, is associated with Judgement. The element of fire is also linked, indicating a spiritual burning ground much like the phoenix rising from the fiery ashes of the furnace of purification.

Judgement — Imagery

This is the resurrection, where the soul survives physical annihilation and is called back to its spiritual homeland.

Judgement embodies the Archangel Gabriel, who like St. Peter, sounds the trumpet of awakening and guides us on our journey toward judgment of our life and its actions, thoughts and deeds.

Judgement is Pluto, Vulcan and Hades, all underworld deities, representing our hellish, unconscious self encountering the archangel of reckoning and receiving absolution.

Judgement is the soul of every person who experiences immortality and acknowledges its survival after the transition called Death. Judgement is life in the Spirit.

Judgement — Interpretation

Upright — Release and transformation.

The Judgement trump represents an increased awareness and use of personal powers. Released from fears and hang-ups, the Seeker is now able to recognize and express his or her will, energy and potentials powerfully and with moral excellence. Psychological transformation into new wholeness and balance between the mind, heart and spirit are the rewards of Judgement.

Release is a major theme of the Judgement trump. The Seeker is liberated from or able to let go of a situation or person. This deliverance may come in the form of a move, change of job or occupation, cure of a health problem or even the release of a loved one.

Following one's own conscience regarding important matters and refusing to allow another's domination are other interpretations of Judgement.

Reversed — Refusal to release, stagnation. Judgement reversed represents the inability to let go of a situation or person.

Fearful of change, the Seeker refuses to accept his own power of control in dealing with an important matter.

Ignoring the advice of one's conscience about changes that are needed creates general stagnation. In medical readings, there could be no cure.

THE WORLD

THE WORLD.

The World — Symbolism

A surprising Saturnian rulership coupled with the image of a gentle dancer are the forces presented in The World card. Also known as The Cosmos or The Universe, The World trump indicates that we are fully aware of who we really are and accept the responsibility of expressing and executing these potentials. A large wreath with semi-hidden Infinity symbols at top and bottom indicate that a victory has matured, a revolution is completed and that life's cycles endlessly begin, culminate and ebb. The wreath's zero-like, shape, reminiscent of The Fool card, hints that a new initiation of events is occurring as the present circumstances are finalized. We begin again in the starting stages of life as The Fool. The idea is that we've learned through the prior experiences and are evolving, producing life accomplishments that are continually spiraling upwards.

The dancer holds two wands to suggest complete purification and control of the conscious and subconscious aspects of the self. All is neutralized, perfected and balanced. Life has become a dedication to the service of a higher master, objective or cause.

The number XXI (21) suggests the individual self has become united with the personal and divine subconscious and has freshly emerged as the self-conscious identity, number one (1), performing the true spiritual dance of life by uniting personal will and world with God's.

The World — Imagery

She is the Greek earth goddess Gaea, whose soil provides sustenance for humankind.

She is the female aspect of Saturn encircled with a victorious wreath for she has learned the true meaning of responsibility and limitation.

She is a karmic goddess of reward, endowing benefit to those who are deserving. She is the cosmic dancer who has discovered and accepted her true self and now performs the dance of "Being."

She is the representation of every person who accepts the responsibility and administrative duties of ruling his or her own personal microcosmic universe.

The World — Interpretation

Upright — Realization of plans. Responsibility.

The World trump assures triumph and prosperity in any reading graced with this final card's presence. It is power and accomplishment coupled with the acceptance of responsibility.

Along with this mastery, the Seeker is learning how to be successful within the limitations of the personal world and its reality and duties. Self- acceptance of both personality assets and flaws creates self-respect, reverence toward all living creatures and a pledge to attain all one can from every life experience.

The World trump symbolizes knowing and expressing oneself and achieving material and familial happiness through this self-expression.

In an employment reading, The World card will often represent administrative work.

World travel is represented as well.

Reversed — Partial victory.

The World reversed suggests that success has not reached the Seeker yet and is still to come. A victory is incomplete.

The World reversed may also pertain to the inability to accept oneself or the responsibilities of life.

Review of the Major Arcana XV-XXI

MATCHING

Upright Meanings

_____ 1. The Devil   a. Breakdown brings transformation.
_____ 2. The Tower   b. Deception or psychic ability.
_____ 3. The Star   c. New, reborn self.
_____ 4. The Moon   d. Responsibility of success.
_____ 5. The Sun   e. Hopes and aspirations.
_____ 6. Judgement   f. Limitations of role-playing.
_____ 7. The World   g. Release and conscience.

Reversed Meanings

_____ 1. The Devil   a. Creative enterprise comes together.
_____ 2. The Tower   b. Partial victory.
_____ 3. The Star   c. Truth reveals selfishness.
_____ 4. The Moon   d. Failure and emptiness.
_____ 5. The Sun   e. Lessons learned brings freedom.
_____ 6. Judgement   f. Talents and aspirations are dashed.
_____ 7. The World   g. Inability to release a situation.

Connect the card with the Character

_____ 1. The Devil   a. The spiritual source calling an individual's soul home.
_____ 2. The Tower   b. The unrealistic or deceptive self.
_____ 3. The Star   c. The fearful, selfish, materialistic person.
_____ 4. The Moon
_____ 5. The Sun   d. The talented-inspired person.
_____ 6. Judgement   e. The newborn, spiritual person.
_____ 7. The World   f. A person awakening to reality.
    g. A well-controlled, successful person.

Answers to Review

MATCHING

Upright Meanings

1. **f**   2. **a**   3. **e**   4. **b**   5. **c**   6. **g**   7. **d**

Reversed Meanings

1. **e**   2. **c**   3. **f**   4. **a**   5. **d**   6. **g**   7. **b**

Connect the word with the Character

1. **c**   2. **f**   3. **d**   4. **b**   5. **e**   6. **a**   7. **g**

Assignment

A reading using the Major Arcana XV-XXI.

Lay out the following reading:

THE INDICATOR
Indicator card — The Emperor

THE CUT
Past — Judgement reversed
Present — Queens of Wands reversed
Future — The Tower

1. Who is The Emperor presently dealing with and what is this individual's behavior?

   _____

   _____

2. The Past reveals Judgement reversed. Explain:

   _____

   _____

   _____

3. The Tower in the Future suggests:

   _____

   _____

   _____

THE READING

Placement 1	Present Influence — The Moon
Placement 2	Helps or Obstacles — The Devil
Placement 3	Past, Motivation — The Star reversed
Placement 4	Recent Past — Page of Swords reversed
Placement 5	Possible Outcome — Four of Pentacles reversed
Placement 6	Immediate Future — Ten of Wands reversed
Placement 7	Seeker's Attitude — Ten of Pentacles
Placement 8	Other's Viewpoint — Three of Pentacles reversed
Placement 9	Hopes and Fears — The World
Placement 10	Final Outcome — Page of Pentacles.

Lay out an eleventh card, The Sun, because a court card has fallen in Placement 10.

BASIC OBSERVATIONS

1. The strongest suit, including the Indicator card, is:

   _____

2. What does this represent? _____

   _____

3. The second most dominant suit is:

   a. _____

   b. suggesting _____ matters.

4. a. How many reversed cards are there? _____

   b. Meaning? _____

   _____

5 a. The numerology of the Reading, excluding the Cut.

   _____

   _____

   b. What does this indicate? _____

   _____

   c. Is the reading dominated by low, middle or high numbers
      of the Major Arcana? _____

   d. Interpret. _____

   _____

   _____

6. The Emperor was chosen for the Indicator card. Describe
   this male Seeker and his concerns:

   _____

   _____

7. What are the forces involved at present in the Seeker's
   question?

   _____

   _____

8. What is now opposing him or causing him adversity?

   _____

   _____

9. What has already happened in their situation?

   _____

   _____

10. The Page of Swords reversed is the Recent Past. Explain.

    _____

    _____

    _____

11. The Four of Pentacles reversed fell in the Possible Future position. Interpret. _____

_____

_____

_____

12. The Ten of Wands reversed foretells what will happen next to the Seeker:

_____

_____

_____

13. The Star reversed and The Tower card have a similar meaning that is very important and revealing in this layout. Refer to the section on Card Combinations (page xxx):

_____

_____

_____

14. What are the father's thoughts? _____

_____

15. How do others see this dilemma? _____

_____

16. Describe his Hopes and Fears.
17. The Page of Pentacles, a Court Card, turned up for his Final Outcome placement. The next card reveals what will happen as a result of the Page of Pentacles. What do you think the two cards together suggest?

_____

_____

_____

Answers to Assignment

A reading using the Major Arcana XV-XXI.

THE CUT

1. In the Present a selfish, demanding, manipulative woman (Queen of Wands reversed) is involved in the Seeker's question. He confirms that he's asking about his relationship with his daughter.
2. Past conditions reveal that the Seeker has lost his own power to this woman. No growth has occurred possibly because of their inability to release an unhappy, unhealthy psychological relationship in the family.
3. The Future brings a crisis point. The truth will prevail. Selfish motivations will be revealed and exposed. He will see the reality of the circumstance.

THE READING

1. The strongest suit is the Major Arcana cards — six.
2. Powerful spiritual and psychological forces govern the reading. The situation may not be fully within the Seeker's or his daughter's control.
3. a. The second most dominant suit is Pentacles.
   b. This suggests money or realistic and practical matters.
4. a. Five are reversed
   b. There is some upset regarding the question
5. a. The reading adds up to 117, reduced to 9.
   b. Achievement concerning personal goals, ideals, emotional matters. Also, attainment and endings.
   c. The reading has two (2) tens.
   d. A conclusion is suggested. This corresponds with the reading's overall numerology.
6. The Seeker is a mature man who approaches his question with reason. He desires control of the situation. Because The Emperor is the father card, the question concerns his relationship to a daughter.
7. The Emperor is now having the wool pulled over his eyes. Forces of falseness and deception prevail. An unexpected turn of events may be occurring.
8. The Devil tells us that he is experiencing manipulative, confining conditions. The daughter may be playing on his fears to take advantage of him.

9. The Star reversed shows a history of unhappiness and disappointment in their relationship. Possibly the reversed Queen of Wands has had poor mental or physical health and has suffered from insecurity which prevented the attainment of hopes and goals.

10. Recently he has been the victim of cruel, manipulative behavior. He may have received a disruptive, upsetting message about her or from her.

11. He could lose his power or authority in handling the situation. He could end up feeling weak and succumb to her. Perhaps he could allow her to take financial advantage of him.

12. More pressure will be applied. Her selfishness will cause her to push him to a breaking point in their relationship. For him this may be ruinous, a final straw. Warn him of these trends, especially because they are reinforced by the Future cut card, The Tower.

13. Both reveal mental health problems. The Star reversed shows depression and anxiety, while breakdowns are signified by the Tower. The reversed Queen of Wands obviously has serious problems.

14. He is thinking about family reputation, his professional standing and insuring financial stability.

15. Family and friends may feel his efforts toward his daughter have brought half-hearted attempts on her part.

16. He hopes that all problems will clear and that and their relationship will succeed.

17. Sometimes life can be progressing in its usual manner when something almost miraculous occurs.

Notice the tremendous difference between the two ending cards and the remainder of the reading.

The Sun trump can cancel any surrounding negativity. It also forecasts a rebirth. The Page of Pentacles suggests some information and advice that will bring about the transformation promised by The Sun. This could be new respect between a father (The Emperor) and his child (Page). A lesson will be learned successfully.

The turning point may come when whatever The Tower creates comes to pass. The truth will then be clear. Upheaval can pave the way for change.

PART IV
SUMMARY

TAROT PRACTICE

The Album

One very creative way to reinforce your knowledge is by making a Tarot album. A large photo album is suitable. Each double page represents a card. Fill the pages with pictures you clip from magazines, newspapers, etc. that represent what each card symbolizes to you. Photographs of paintings, poems, phrases and sayings may also be included. Over the years you can add to the preliminary pictures you've placed in your album, creating a beautiful, lasting personal Tarot treasury.

Tarot Practice

The main objective of this lesson is to introduce you to the many creative aspects of Tarot. The cards, because they represent our life can be discovered everywhere, much like a Tarot treasure hunt!

When reading a book you can think of the characters and their situations as the Court, Major and Minor Arcana. The same practice applies to movies, television, newspaper articles, even Ann Landers! All consist of three main categories, persons, events and morals. Try these exercises to heighten your sensitivity and add to your Tarot knowledge.

A Tarot costume party is always fun, especially because you are learning the cards in a group atmosphere. The participants dress as characters from the cards, basically the Major Arcana.

Charades, where one individual acts out a card and a group of people try to guess its identity is also a learning tool.

Let us look back, at this point on our journey, to when we first embarked on our Tarot study. Turn to page xvi where your first Tarot favorites and dislikes were recorded. Can you see what your instinctive selections were telling you? Recognize how far you've come! Remember those strange looking symbols and numbers? They don't seem so strange anymore, you've learned a new and valuable language that transcends Tarot cards in its scope. Art can be interpreted in a deep, insightful manner by using the new Tarot language you've acquired. You may even find paintings depicting Tarot cards themselves, especially from the Medieval Era and pre-Raphaelite school of art.

Tarot is a picture of life. People are portrayed by the Court Cards, the daily events are depicted by the Minor Arcana, and the lessons and philosophy are represented by the Major Arcana.

It is important for us to begin to live and breathe Tarot, finding its fascinating and totally encompassing philosophy in all we see and do. For example, at the present time as I write this manuscript I feel I am the Eight of Pentacles, an apprentice to the field of book writing. When I complete my manuscript and see my work published successfully I will be the Three of Pentacles and The Sun trump. The Three of Pentacles depicts the master receiving reward and recognition for the accomplished work. The Sun trump indicates achievement and successful completion of a venture. On another level I could already be considered as the Three of Pentacles in the Tarot Card field. I began as an apprentice as you presently are, working hard, sincerely trying and experiencing some success.

Almost everything in our lives can be characterized by a Tarot card or two. The idea is to personally animate the card by making them a part of all you do.

Assignment

Describe your day by laying out the appropriate Tarot cards in sequence. You may want to share this exercise with a friend or loved one or with a fellow Tarot card student. This is a unique way of relating and communicating with someone. If this person is unfamiliar with Tarot they can use this book to interpret your day through the cards. This assignment is vital in helping you think in Tarot card terms, therefore reinforcing your knowledge, usage and interpretation of the cards. Do this assignment for one week. Remember to include how you felt and thought as well as the people in your day and the actions that you took.

Example

APRIL 10, 1982 SATURDAY MORNING

I woke early and finished writing a letter for a job application. Additionally, I composed a rough draft of a letter following up a second potential job prospect that an editor had expressed interest in but couldn't use at the moment. I felt creative and ambitious this morning. Translation into Tarot: The Empress and the Queen of Wands — I was feeling creative and ambitious, desirous of making more of my potentials.

The Magician and the Two of Wands. Translation: I had a creative idea that I turned into a business proposal. I created the idea, organized my thoughts and wrote them in letter form. You can see how The Magician represents having a creative idea and organizing it to make it become real. The Two of Wands tells us that my idea is pertaining to something sincere and is in the initial stages. I cast the idea out in the form of a letter of inquiry and await results.

The Four of Swords reversed indicates the reactivation of something that has been shelved, therefore, the second letter of inquiry to the editor I had previously dealt with. The editor is characterized as the Queen of Swords for she is a professional woman who exercises decision-making power over the matter.

THE AFTERNOON

The afternoon hours were decidedly different from the morning hours. The scene changed to family and domesticity as the laundry was done and I purchased a birthday gift for my boyfriend. The Easter bunny came one day early when I distributed holiday chocolate to my boyfriend's family. A close friend called late in the afternoon. We discussed some business plans and her graduation party. Translation into Tarot: During the afternoon I was repeatedly reminded of the Six of Cups. Most of the afternoon was spent giving presents, visiting family and talking with friends. The Eight of Wands describes my successful and quick accomplishment of a goal — the laundry, which I achieved through a short trip.

The Knight of Wands, Six of Pentacles and the Six of Cups. Translation: The Six of Pentacles describes the giving of a gift as does the Six of Cups e.g., sharing with a loved one. The Six of Pentacles reminded of the kind of purchase and how I felt about it because the gift was an investment in my boyfriend's future; the Knight of Wands' career plans. The gift has the quality of benefitting the recipient and the giver. The Six of Cups is again interpreted as the Easter chocolate given to the family.

The Page of Wands, the Queen of Wands, the Three of Pentacles, The Sun and the Six of Cups again! Translation: My girlfriend phoned me with good news, she was getting feedback pertaining to some of her original ideas, others were cooperating by supplying information and becoming part of her team. An influential person has also affiliated with her cause. The whole situation is clearly described by the Three of Wands. We discussed her graduation, the Three of Pentacles and The Sun, and the date of the party, the Four of Wands. This card symbolizes the occasion because of the concept of completed work celebrated. The Three of Cups also applies as it represents a happy ending. The Six of Cups again appeared as she told me what she wanted for her graduation present!

THE EVENING
The evening was quiet. I prepared a birthday dinner for my boyfriend as part of his present; there's that Six of Cups again! We watched television with his father. The Six of Cups describes the domestic scene as well as the reunion with a family member, in this case his father or The Emperor trump.

In this diary you may also include how you slept and what you dreamt.

As you spend the week laying out the cards for each day you will see an interesting pattern begin to emerge. Keep a record of the week and then analyze it. Look especially for clusterings of one suit or type of activity and the absence of others.

Analysis

Analyze your week by asking yourself the following questions.
1. How much time was spent on others compared to time spent on yourself? For example, my sample day devoted one third to my own personal pursuits and two-thirds to domestic pursuits and sharing with others.
2. How much did you give compared to what you received?
3. What suits dominated? For example a large number of Wands and Swords and very little in Cups would indicate a need for more family, emotional, loving and feeling activity in your life. What you can do to bring a balance is as simple as laying out the suit of Cups and choosing one of the cards as a goal to be achieved.

4. Major Arcana. Were there few Majors, suggesting a preoccupation with the daily routine at the expense of focusing on the deeper
   side of yourself? Many Major Arcana indicate self-awareness on
   a spiritual, psychological and philosophical life level. Too many
   or an overabundance of Majors can indicate too much time spent
   in the higher, mental worlds and not enough on the basic physical plane of practicality and responsibility.
5. People. What amount of Court cards were present? Did you have
   many people and a healthy variety influencing your week? Too
   many may indicate lack of time for rest and personal pursuits.
   Not enough symbolizes the need to get out and socialize.
6. Compare time spent in mental versus physical pursuits, emotional
   versus intellectual, financial versus leisure, etc.
7. Compare time spent actively versus passively.

In Summary

By discovering what is missing you can associate that topic to one
of the four suits, Court cards or Major Arcana. By allocating the missing element to its proper suit you can discover how to remedy and
rebalance your life. Lay out the corresponding deficient suit, Major
Arcanas or Court cards and ponder how you could incorporate the
circumstances portrayed in the cards into your life.

KEYWORDS — THE MINOR ARCANA NUMBER CARDS

Aces

ACE OF WANDS
Astrological Key: Fire
Symbolizes the desire, will and drive of Aries, Leo and Sagittarius.

Upright — Beginning of desire, ambition, idea or venture.

Reversed — A new start encounters difficulties, pressures.

ACE OF CUPS
Astrological Key: Water
Exemplifies the emotional nature of Pisces, Cancer and Scorpio.

Upright — The onstart of a situation of loving, understanding, self-understanding, inspirational, or spiritual feelings.

Reversed — Blocked communication of feelings with others or even within one's self.

ACE OF SWORDS
Astrological Key: Air
Displays the powerful minds and actions of Gemini, Libra and Aquarius.

Upright — Winning through fair actions and mental willpower.

Reversed — Unconquerable difficulties (for the time being). Don't push.

ACE OF PENTACLES
Astrological Key: Earth
Earth and Pentacles express the realism and solidity of Taurus, Virgo and Capricorn.

Upright — A plan becomes real. New money and security.

Reversed — Plans do not work out. Money is tight or tightness with money.

Twos

TWO OF WANDS
Astrological Keys: Fire, Aries, Leo and Sagittarius
This suit blends with the idea of the number two's meaning of Balance.

Upright — Waiting for results concerning an important desire or goal.

Reversed — Little or nothing transpires concerning the goal. Frustration.

TWO OF CUPS
Astrological Keys: Water, Cancer, Scorpio and Pisces

Upright — Balanced sharing in a relationship. Any balance.

Reversed — Unbalanced relationship. Inner imbalance or disharmony.

TWO OF SWORDS
Astrological Keys: Air, Gemini, Libra and Aquarius

Upright — Postponement of decisions, unresolved question, inaction.

Reversed — Action and decision making.

TWO OF PENTACLES
Astrological Keys: Earth, Taurus, Virgo and Capricorn

Upright — Adapting to change. Alterations. Balancing money and financial obligations. Employment changes.

Reversed — Inability to handle responsibilities, loss of financial balance. Changes bring difficulties.

Threes

THREE OF WANDS
Astrological Keys: Fire, Aries, Leo and Sagittarius

Upright — Growth. Working together brings positive results.

Reversed — No growth, poor results.

THREE OF CUPS
Astrological Keys: Water, Cancer, Scorpio and Pisces

Upright — Happy endings. Growth and promises in romance.

Reversed — Spoiled romance, unhappy endings.

THREE OF SWORDS
Astrological Keys: Air, Gemini, Libra and Aquarius

Upright — Endings, severances, separations (sometimes for the good).

Reversed — Less intense pain concerning separations or severances.

THREE OF PENTACLES
Astrological Keys: Earth, Taurus, Virgo and Capricorn

Upright — Excellence brings merits and tangible rewards.

Reversed — Half-hearted attempts lead to ordinary results.

Fours

FOUR OF WANDS
Astrological Keys: Fire, Aries, Leo and Sagittarius

Upright — Happiness, harmony and established, secure victory.

Reversed — Blessings, protection and victory.

FOUR OF CUPS
Astrological Keys: Water, Cancer, Scorpio and Pisces

Upright — Questioning the old and consideration of the new. Emotional withdrawal. Contemplation.

Reversed — Flowing with and acting upon feelings. Relationships begin, change or evolve.

FOUR OF SWORDS
Astrological Keys: Air, Gemini, Libra and Aquarius

Upright — Withdrawal. Battle fatigue. Truce, resting, meditation, vacation.

Reversed — Returning to the rigors of life. Renewal of shelved interest or pursuit.

FOUR OF PENTACLES
Astrological Keys: Earth, Taurus, Virgo and Capricorn

Upright — Successful and secure job and economic position. Can also be an inability to trust, give and share when cards of selfishness are present.

Reversed — Loss of power, position, control or money.

Fives

FIVE OF WANDS
Astrological Keys: Fire, Aries, Leo and Sagittarius

Upright — Inner or outer fighting. Self-defense. Strength in facing adverse or testing conditions.

Reversed — Eliminating or changing of outworn ways of handling things result in new harmony and tranquility.

FIVE OF CUPS
Astrological Keys: Water, Cancer, Scorpio and Pisces

Upright — Emotional losses. Accentuate assets rather than dwell on what has already been spilt.

Reversed — New hopes for reunions, reconciliations and reappearances in the Seeker's emotional life.

FIVE OF SWORDS
Astrological Keys: Air, Gemini, Libra and Aquarius

Upright — Cruel words, hurtful actions used in defeating others or one's self. Revengeful goals are meaningless and demeaning.

Reversed — The same.

FIVE OF PENTACLES
Astrological Keys: Earth, Taurus, Virgo and Capricorn

Upright — Depression, deprivation and poverty. Loss.

Reversed — Better times, hopefulness, new income.

Sixes

SIX OF WANDS
Astrological Keys: Fire, Aries, Leo and Sagittarius

Upright — Winning through sincerity, ambition and perseverance.

Reversed — Losing to another. "Second fiddle." Delayed success.

SIX OF CUPS
Astrological Keys: Water, Cancer, Scorpio and Pisces

Upright — Cherished harmony in relationships and domestic life.

Reversed — Unproductively dwelling on unhappy past memories. Leave them behind.

SIX OF SWORDS
Astrological Keys: Air, Gemini, Libra and Aquarius

Upright — Circumstances and attitudes change for the better. Conditions improve.

Reversed — Problems remain. Attitude change may help.

SIX OF PENTACLES
Astrological Keys: Earth, Taurus, Virgo and Capricorn

Upright — Sharing. Receiving well deserved profits. Successful balance of money matters.

Reversed — Unbalanced, unjust moneys. Loss or unscrupulous dealings.

Sevens

SEVEN OF WANDS
Astrological Keys: Fire, Aries, Leo and Sagittarius

Upright — Uses courage and sincerity of purpose to confront circumstances. Confrontation.

Reversed — No confrontation.

SEVEN OF CUPS
Astrological Keys: Water, Cancer, Scorpio and Pisces

Upright — Indecision, fantasizing, delusions.

Reversed — A new goal is chosen. Decisiveness.

SEVEN OF SWORDS
Astrological Keys: Air, Gemini, Libra and Aquarius

Upright — Unfairly stealing or cheating oneself or others.

Reversed — Receiving or making an apology. Being your own best friend.

SEVEN OF PENTACLES
Astrological Keys: Earth, Taurus, Virgo and Capricorn

Upright — Reassessment after much effort. Incompleteness.

Reversed — Worries concerning practical matters.

Eights

EIGHT OF WANDS
Astrological Keys: Fire, Aries, Leo and Sagittarius

Upright — The "Green Light" or "Go Ahead" card.

Reversed — Stop, don't force a situation.

EIGHT OF CUPS
Astrological Keys: Water, Cancer, Scorpio and Pisces

Upright — Withdrawal, disappointment, searching.

Reversed — Enjoyment of the emotional, domestic and social aspects of life.

EIGHT OF SWORDS
Astrological Keys: Air, Gemini, Libra and Aquarius

Upright — Restriction and interference from self or others.

Reversed — Action, freedom.

EIGHT OF PENTACLES
Astrological Keys: Earth, Taurus, Virgo and Capricorn

Upright — "Working on it," learning, training.

Reversed — Misuse of abilities and cleverness.

Nines

NINE OF WANDS
Astrological Keys: Fire, Aries, Leo and Sagittarius

Upright — Get ready, remain on the defensive for problems will reoccur.

Reversed — Caught off guard, be on the alert.

NINE OF CUPS
Astrological Keys: Water, Cancer, Scorpio and Pisces

Upright — Happiness, wishes and hopes come true.

Reversed — Excessive spending, self-indulgence, disappointments.

NINE OF SWORDS
Astrological Keys: Air, Gemini, Libra and Aquarius

Upright — Torment in both the life and the mind.

Reversed — Improved, balanced conditions.

NINE OF PENTACLES
Astrological Keys: Earth, Taurus, Virgo and Capricorn

Upright — Independence, wisdom, self-confidence, financial gains.

Reversed — Financial and personal losses and "insecurities."

Tens

TEN OF WANDS
Astrological Keys: Fire, Aries, Leo and Sagittarius

Upright — Hardship weighed down. Some failures due to overextending oneself.

Reversed — Failures caused deliberately.

TEN OF CUPS
Astrological Keys: Water, Cancer, Scorpio and Pisces

Upright — Satisfaction, protection, and completion.

Reversed — Dissatisfaction, disagreements, and incompleteness.

TEN OF SWORDS
Astrological Keys: Air, Gemini, Libra and Aquarius

Upright — Plans fail.

Reversed — Restoration of hope, spiritual help.

TEN OF PENTACLES
Astrological Keys: Earth, Taurus, Virgo and Capricorn

Upright — Financial abundance. Transition resulting from life's natural progression.

Reversed — Financial and/or family complications and instability.

KEYWORDS — THE MINOR ARCANA COURT CARDS

Pages

PAGE OF WANDS

Astrological Keys: Fire, Aries, Leo and Sagittarius

Upright — Characteristics of leadership and attention loving.
Message: Sudden good news.

Reversed — Characteristics of theatrics and troublesome behavior.
Message: Unfortunate news may be over-dramatized.

PAGE OF CUPS

Astrological Keys: Water, Cancer, Scorpio and Pisces

Upright — Character: Sensitive and imaginative.
Message: Inspirational, uplifting; may come from own subconscious,
(i.e. dream).

Reversed — Character: Emotional and socially immature,
daydreamer.
Message: Ignoring internal psychic messages.

PAGE OF SWORDS

Astrological Keys: Air, Gemini, Libra and Aquarius

Upright — Character: Communicative, intelligent and clever.
Message: Unexpected upset.

Reversed — Character: Cruel, manipulating and calculating.
Message: Disruptive, upsetting news.

PAGE OF PENTACLES

Astrological Keys: Earth, Taurus, Virgo and Capricorn

Upright — Character: Studious, responsible and careful.
Message: Informative, advisory.

Reversed — Character: Dislikes authority, is careless and uncompromising.
Message: Disregarding or disrespecting information or advice.

Knights

KNIGHT OF WANDS
Astrological Keys: Fire, Aries, Leo and Sagittarius

Upright — Character: Warm, friendly and ambitious.
Event: Has an important nature pertaining to one's desires or goals.

Reversed — Character: Self-centered, demanding and arrogant.
Event: Employment disruptions.

KNIGHT OF CUPS
Astrological Keys: Water, Cancer, Scorpio and Pisces

Upright — Character: Imaginative, sincere and romantic.
Event: Has a significant emotional or romantic theme.

Reversed — Character: Deceptive within self and with others. Not facing the facts.
Event: Concerning unrealistic deceptiveness.

KNIGHT OF SWORDS
Astrological Keys: Air, Gemini, Libra and Aquarius

Upright — Character: Intelligent, persuasive and an intellectual.
Event: A sudden arrival or occurrence.

Reversed — Character: Dictatorial, unfairly accusatory, verbal and mental game playing. Interfering.
Event: A situation or person suddenly or unexpectedly departs.

KNIGHT OF PENTACLES
Astrological Keys: Earth, Taurus, Virgo and Capricorn

Upright — Character: Stable, hardworking, money minded.
Event: Concerning finance, possessions, property or employment.

Reversed — Character: Careless and impractical concerning money, property or employment.
Event: Unstable position, money or job.

Queens

QUEEN OF WANDS
Astrological Keys: Fire, Aries, Leo and Sagittarius

Upright — Attractive personality, warm and powerful.

Reversed — Selfish, demanding, envious.

QUEEN OF CUPS
Astrological Keys: Water, Cancer, Scorpio and Pisces

Upright — Loving, sympathetic and intuitive.

Reversed — Overly sensitive, unrealistic; worries, fears and unfulfilled dreams dominate her thoughts.

QUEEN OF SWORDS
Astrological Keys: Air, Gemini, Libra and Aquarius

Upright — Intelligent, independent, decisive and analytical.

Reversed — Bitter, sarcastic and severely judgmental.

QUEEN OF PENTACLES
Astrological Keys: Earth, Taurus, Virgo and Capricorn

Upright — Sensible, caring and productive.

Reversed — Unrealistic, insecure and very dependent.

Kings

KING OF WANDS
Astrological Keys: Fire, Aries, Leo and Sagittarius

Upright — Personable, ambitious and leadership characteristics.

Reversed — Selfish, dominating and argumentative.

KING OF CUPS
Astrological Keys: Water, Cancer, Scorpio and Pisces

Upright — Sensitive, intelligent, deep feeling nature.

Reversed — Deceptive, inconstant, emotionally weak or disturbed.

KING OF SWORDS
Astrological Keys: Air, Gemini, Libra and Aquarius

Upright — Intellectual, decisive, fair-minded. Can be a decision fairly rendered.

Reversed — Unfair, cruel and prejudiced. Can indicate an unfair decision.

KING OF PENTACLES
Astrological Keys: Earth, Taurus, Virgo, Capricorn

Upright — Realistic, materialistic, security conscious.

Reversed — Stubborn, excessively money conscious, possessive.

KEYWORDS —
THE MAJOR ARCANA

0 THE FOOL
Planet: Uranus — Color: Light Yellow

Upright — Major decisions, potentials and favorable circumstances. Important life option is presented to or initiated by the Seeker.

Reversed — Foolishness, wrong selections, not thinking before acting.

1 THE MAGICIAN
Planet: Mercury — Color: Yellow

Upright — Planning, establishment or working out of an idea, focusing and concentrating on a goal, ambition or plan.

Reversed — Manipulation, unrealized projects and ambitions.

2 THE HIGH PRIESTESS
Planet: Moon — Color: Blue

Upright — Changes often positive, unknown factors. Secretive, psychic, mystical, spiritual woman. Apply high ideals and morals in handling the question.

Reversed — Unsuspected problems may bring negative changes. Bitter, unhappy woman.

3 THE EMPRESS
Planet: Venus — Color: Green

Upright — The ability to give and receive love. Creativity, growth, happiness and abundance. May symbolize a woman of these qualities along with independence, domestic and financial prosperity. Successful manager and ruler.

Reversed — Inability to give or receive love, emotional problems. No growth.

4   **THE EMPEROR**
Astrological Key: Aries — Color: Red

Upright — Manifested results. Mature, independent, sensible and intelligent.

Reversed — Plans disintegrate. Inconstant, unreasonable, dependent man.

5   **THE HIEROPHANT**
Astrological Key: Taurus — Color: Red Orange

Upright — Usual, customary or traditional approach. A teacher. Intuition.

Reversed — May represent an unusual person who is a "character." Ignoring intuition. Unique, different or unusual approach to a circumstance.

6   **THE LOVERS**
Astrological Key: Gemini — Color: Orange

Upright — Correct selection, successful communication. Healing. Balance.

Reversed — Incorrect selection, poor healing, difficulties in communication, meddling.

7   **THE CHARIOT**
Astrological Key: Cancer — Color: Amber

Upright — Balance through self-control. Successful speaking.

Reversed — Loss of self-control, defeat.

8   **STRENGTH**
Astrological Key: Leo — Color: Yellow Gold

Upright — Spiritual lovingness. Self-understanding and acceptance. Use psychological awareness for control.

Reversed — Lack of self-acceptance and understanding leads to selfishness and being overcome with negative emotions, hatefulness, greed and violence. Psychological illness.

9 ## THE HERMIT
Astrological Key: Virgo — Color: Yellow Green

Upright — Advice, recommendations, guidance from within. Attainment. Instructor.

Reversed — Inability to learn from past mistakes. Ignoring counsel. An unwise action.

10 ## WHEEL OF FORTUNE
Astrological Key: Jupiter — Color: Royal Blue

Upright — Be prepared for opportunity. Rewards, good timing.

Reversed — Poor timing, reoccurring problems, delays and hindrances.

11 ## JUSTICE
Astrological Key: Libra — Color: Green

Upright — Important decision made with conviction, strength and correctness. Balance. Action. Education. Fair or just rewards.

Reversed — Unfairness. Actions may be too rigid or uncompromising.

12 ## THE HANGED MAN
Astrological Key: Neptune — Color: Green Blue

Upright — Change in priorities, forfeiting something in order to attain something better.

Reversed — Selfishness, pride and egotism prevents the Seeker from letting a situation unfold as it should. Inability to change or listen to another viewpoint.

13 ## DEATH
Astrological Key: Scorpio — Color: Blue Green

Upright — Fresh start, liberating change. Growth toward a new or different direction for the better.

Reversed — Inactivity, no movement, impermanent standstill.

♏ TEMPERANCE
Astrological Key: Sagittarius — Color: Deep Blue

Upright — Successful handling of a situation. Adjusting and balancing. Good timing. Tests passed.

Reversed — Becoming "carried away;" overdoing or excessiveness in behavior. Disorganized, improper or poor managing of a situation. Wrong timing. Tests failed.

♑ THE DEVIL
Astrological Key: Capricorn — Color: Indigo

Upright — Enslavement, confining restrictive conditions. Overwhelming fear of real or imagined enemy or opposition. Power mongering.

Reversed — Freedom from fears, enslavements and internal or external enemies.

♈ THE TOWER
Astrological Key: Mars — Color: Red

Upright — Truth and reality, sometimes unexpectedly. A situation reaches a point of crisis or warfare. Prevailing structures are altered or changed.

Reversed — A situation is seen in the light of reality. A manageable crisis, expected changes.

♒ THE STAR
Astrological attribution: Aquarius — Color: Violet

Upright — Focusing energy on the pursuit of wishes, talents, dreams and goals. Meditation. Good health.

Reversed — Disappointments. Inability to pursue dreams, talents or goals. Depression and insecurity. Poor attitude.

♓ THE MOON
Astrological attribution: Pisces — Color: Violet Red

Upright — Falseness, hidden factors, unexpected turn of events.

Reversed — Honesty, positive growth and changes. New harmony.

THE SUN

Astrological attribution: Sun — Color: Gold

Upright — Victory, rebirth, protection.

Reversed — Defeat and emptiness. Unsuccessful.

JUDGEMENT

Astrological attribution: Pluto — Color: Red Orange

Upright — Release, transformation, awareness of own personal power. Positive, important change.

Reversed — Loss of power to others. Inability to release. No change.

THE WORLD

Astrological attribution: Saturn — Color: Indigo Blue

Upright — Attainment. Accomplishment coupled with acceptance of responsibility.

Reversed — Partial, incomplete or unfinished project. Minor progress but no victory yet.

Bibliography

Calvino, Italo. *The Castle of Crossed Destinies*. New York: Harcourt Brace Jovanovich, 1977.

Case, Paul Foster. *The Book of Tokens, Tarot Meditations*. Calif.: Builders of Adytum, 1934.

_____. *Highlights of Tarot*. Los Angeles: Builders of Adytum, 1931.

_____. *The Tarot, A Key to the Wisdom of the Ages*. Virginia: Macoy Publishers, 1927.

Cavendish, Richard. *The Tarot*. New York, 1975.

Cirlot, Juan Eduardo. *A Dictionary of Symbols*. New York, 1972.

Cooke, John and Rosalind Sharpe. *The New Tarot*. Kentfield, Calif., 1968.

Crowley, Aliester. *The Book of Thoth*. New York: Weiser, 1944.

Davidson, Gustav. *A Dictionary of Angels*. New York: Free Press, 1972.

Douglas, Alfred. *The Tarot, The Origins, Meanings and Uses of the Cards*. New York: Penquin, 1972.

Douglas, Nik and Penny Slinger. *Secret Dakini Oracle*. New York: Inner Tradition, 1979.

Fortune, Dion. *The Mystical Qabalah*. London: Weiser, 1984.

Gray, Eden. *Mastering the Tarot*. New York: New American Library, 1971.

Haich, Elisabeth. *Wisdom of the Tarot*. New York: Aurora Press, 1975.

Hoeller, Stephen. *The Royal Road*. Wheaton, Ill.: Theosophical Publishing House, 1975.

Holy Order of Mans. *Jewels of the Wise*. San Francisco: Epiphany Press, 1974.

Javane, Faith and Dusty Bunker. *Numerology and the Divine Triangle*. Gloucester, Mass.: Para Research, 1980.

Kaplan, Stuart R. *The Encyclopedia of Tarot*, Vol. 1. New York: U.S. Games Systems, Inc., 1978.

Knight, Gareth. *A Practical Guide to Qabalistic Symbolism*, 2 vols. New York: Weiser, 1978.

Regardie, Israel. *A Garden of Pomegranates*. St. Paul, Minn.: Llewellyn Publishing, 1970.

Walker, Barbara. *The Womens Encyclopedia of Myths and Secrets*. San Francisco: Harper and Row, 1983.

Index

INFORMATION NEEDED FOR PERSONAL READING

$35.00 Full Price (Money Order or Cashiers Check)

Follow the steps below, copying the layout and filling in with the names of the cards you turn up in your spread.

Using your own personal Tarot deck, choose a question and lay out the reading. See Lesson 3, page 19 of this book.

Step One — Consider your question carefully. You may want to ask about something in your immediate future. This would be difficult because of the time factor involved in my answering your query.

Step Two — Choose a question that will be unfolding over and beyond the next six month period. Example: You can ask —

1. What will happen with my health situation within the next six months?

2. What do I need to understand to improve my health?

3. Show me the circumstances surrounding my health in the future.

Do not ask —

1. How will my health checkup go next week?

2. Will I be healthier soon? (cannot answer a yes or no wording of a question.

Name _____ Date _____

Address _____

_____

Question _____

Step Three — FILL IN CHART:

Indicator Card _____

| | | 10 | 11 |

5

Possible Future

10
Final
Outcome

11
Layout
Card 11
if Card 10
is a Court Card

9

4

1

6

Recent Event
(a couple of
months)

Present Influence

Immediate
Future

9
Hopes &
Fears

2

Helps & Hindrances
Present

8

CUT

3

1. Environment
—home or work
2. How others
see you in the
situation

7

Label Past,
Present and
Future as well
as what top
card is.

Past

On your mind
Mental Outlook
How you see it.

Additional comments: _____

_____

_____

I have enclosed my $35.00 ☐ cashiers check   or   ☐ money order —
plus a stamped self-addressed envelope.

TAROT TRUTHS

The insights and wisdom revealed by the tarot are available to you! Order your own tarot interpretation for **love, work** or **general information**. Our *Timely Tarot* text is written by Kooch Daniels, a professional tarot reader from northern California. Her focus is on using the tarot as a tool for personal transformation and life enhancement.

A choice of four spreads is available:
(1) the classic Celtic Cross, (2) the 12-house Horoscope Spread, (3) the 15-card Future Horoscope Spread or (4) the 24-card Progressed Horoscope Spread.

You can send your own spread (using one of the three layouts mentioned), or ask our computer to generate a spread for you. Astro's high-speed computer compiles the interpretation from text written by Kooch, according to her instructions.

Please specify as to whether your *Timely Tarot* is to be **general** reading, or focused on **love** or **work**.

Our *Timely Tarot* interpretations run 6-12 pages. Prices are listed below. Use our toll-free order lines to charge your *Timely Tarot* by VISA or MasterCard.

To order by telephone: **1-800-826-1085**. Call between 6 AM and 8 PM, Pacific Time. Ask for Dept. TT988. Your bill will include a $2.00 postage and handling charge plus a $2.00 phone charge.

To order by **mail**, provide all the following information to Astro Computing Services, Dept. TT988. Enclose a check or money order for the appropriate amount — plus $2.00 for postage and handling.

I want a *Timely Tarot* for: ☐ general ☐ love ☐ work
Please use the (check one):
Celtic Spread (10 card layout) _____ ($8.00)
Horoscope Spread (12 card layout) _____ ($8.00)
Future Horoscope Spread (15 card layout) _____ ($8.00)
Progressed Horoscope Spread (24 card layout) _____ ($12.00)
I want the computer to generate a spread for me: ☐ yes ☐ no

If "NO" is checked above, please write down the cards for the spread you created, which you want analyzed. (Please use the following abbreviations: C for Cups, S for Swords, P for Pentacles and W for Wands; Pg for Page, Kn for Knight, Q for Queen and K for King; 1-10 for Ace through 10. For the Major Arcana, please write the first four letters of each one, e.g., Fool would be Fool; Justice would be Just; Hanged Man would be Hang, etc. The basic reference as far as names will be the Waite Tarot deck.)

Card #1____   Card #2____   Card #3____   Card #4____   Card #5____
Card #6____   Card #7____   Card #8____   Card #9____   Card #10____
(End here for Celtic Spread)
Card #11____   Card #12____   (End here for Horoscope Spread)
Card #13____   Card #14____   Card #15____   (End here for Future Horoscope)
Card #16____   Card #17____
Card #18____   Card #19____   Card #20____   Card #21____
Card #22____   Card #23____   Card #24____   (Progressed Horoscope)

FAST SERVICE!   **RECEIVED TODAY — MAILED TOMORROW**
Use Your Visa or MasterCard

For mail orders please send check or money order (US dollars) to:

ASTRO COMPUTING SERVICES, DEPT. TT988 • PO BOX 34487 • SAN DIEGO, CA 92103-0802
THE MOST RESPECTED NAME IN ASTROLOGY